MOTHER TERESA
A BIOGRAPHY

MOTHER TERESA
A BIOGRAPHY

by

ILEEN BAER

Alpha Editons

Copyright © 2015

ISBN   :   978-93-85505-33-1

Design and Setting By
Alpha Editions
email - alphaedis@gmail.com

All rights reserved. No part of this publication may be reproduced, distributed, or transmitted in any form or by means, including photocopying, recording, or other electronic or mechanical methods, without the prior written permission of the publisher.

The views and characters expressed in the book are of the author and his/her imagination and do not represent the views of the Publisher.

Contents

	Preface	*(vii)*
1.	Biography	1
2.	Early Life of Mother Teresa	35
3.	Criticism of Mother Teresa	61
4.	Legacy of Mother Teresa	91
5.	Mother Teresa in Calcutta	103
6.	The Macedonian Slavs and Mother Teresa	115
7.	Prayer for a Deceased Person	135
8.	Mother Teresa and Media	155
	Bibliography	170
	Index	171

Preface

Mother Teresa was born, 1910, in Skopje, capital of the Republic of Macedonia. Little is known about her early life, but at a young age she felt a calling to be a nun and serve through helping the poor. At the age of 18 she was given permission to join a group of nuns in Ireland. After a few months of training, with the Sisters of Loreto, she was then given permission to travel to India. She took her formal religious vows in 1931, and chose to be named after St Therese of Lisieux – the patron saint of missionaries.

On 10 September 1946, Teresa experienced what she later described as "the call within the call" while travelling by train to the Loreto convent in Darjeeling from Calcutta for her annual retreat. "I was to leave the convent and help the poor while living among them. It was an order. To fail would have been to break the faith." One author later observed, "Though no one knew it at the time, Sister Teresa had just become *Mother* Teresa".

On her arrival in India, she began by working as a teacher, however the widespread poverty of Calcutta made a deep impression on her; and this led to her starting a new order called "The Missionaries of Charity". The primary objective of this mission was to look after people, who nobody else was prepared to look after. Mother Teresa felt that serving others was a key principle of the teachings of Jesus Christ.

Mother Teresa founded the Missionaries of Charity, a Roman Catholic religious congregation, which in 2012 consisted of over 4,500 sisters and is active in 133 countries.

— Editor

Biography

BlessedT eresa of Calcutta,M C, c ommonly known asM other Teresa (26 August 1910 – 5 September 1997), was a Roman Catholic religious sister and missionary who lived most of her life in India. She was born in today's Macedonia, with her family being of Albanian descent originating in Kosovo.

Mother Teresa founded the Missionaries of Charity, a Roman Catholic religious congregation, which in 2012 consisted of over 4,500 sisters and is active in 133 countries. They run hospices and homes for people with HIV/AIDS, leprosy and tuberculosis; soup kitchens; dispensaries and mobile clinics; children's and family counselling programmes; orphanages; and schools. Members must adhere to the vows of chastity, poverty and obedience as well as a fourth vow, to give "wholehearted free service to the poorest of the poor".

Mother Teresa was the recipient of numerous honours including the 1979 Nobel Peace Prize. In 2003, she was beatified as "Blessed Teresa of Calcutta". A second miracle credited to her intercession is required before she can be recognised as a saint by the Catholic Church.

A controversial figure both during her life and after her death, Mother Teresa was widely admired by many for her charitable works, but also widely criticised, particularly for her efforts opposing contraception and for substandard conditions in the hospices for which she was responsible.

EARLY LIFE

An ethnic Albanian born Anjezë Gonxhe Bojaxhiu (*gonxha* meaning "rosebud" or "little flower" inAlbanian) on 26 August 1910, she considered 27 August, the day she was baptised, to be her "true birthday". Her birthplace of Skopje, now capital

2 *Mother Teresa*

of the Republic of Macedonia, was at the time part of the Ottoman Empire. Her family continued to live in Skopje until 1934, when they moved to Tirana in Albania.

She was the youngest of the children of Nikollë and Dranafile Bojaxhiu (Bernai). Her father, who was involved in Albanian politics, died in 1919 when she was eight years old. Her father may have been fromPr izren,K osovow hile her mother may have been from a village near Yakova.

According to a biography written by Joan Graff Clucas, in her early years Agnes was fascinated by stories of the lives of missionaries and their service in Bengal, and by age 12 had become convinced that she should commit herself to a religious life. Her final resolution was taken on 15 August 1928, while praying at the shrine of the Black Madonna of Letnice, where she often went on pilgrimage.

She left home at age 18 to join the Sisters of Loreto as a missionary. She never again saw her mother or sister.

Agnes initially went to the Loreto Abbey in Rathfarnham, Ireland, to learn English, the language the Sisters of Loreto used to teach school children in India. She arrived in India in 1929, and began her novitiate in Darjeeling, near the Himalayan mountains, where she learnt Bengali and taught at the St. Teresa's School, a schoolhouse close to her convent. She took her first religious vows as a nun on 24 May 1931. At that time she chose to be named after Thérèse de Lisieux, the patron saint of missionaries, but because one nun in the convent had already chosen that name, Agnes opted for the Spanish spelling*Teresa*.

She took her solemn vows on 14 May 1937, while serving as a teacher at the Loreto convent school in Entally, eastern Calcutta. Teresa served there for almost twenty years and in 1944 was appointed headmistress.

Although Teresa enjoyed teaching at the school, she was increasingly disturbed by the poverty surrounding her inC alcutta(Kolkata). T heB engal famine of 1943b rought misery and death to the city; and the outbreak of Hindu/Muslim violence in August 1946 plunged the city into despair and horror.

Biography 3

MISSIONARIES OF CHARITY

On 10 September 1946, Teresa experienced what she later described as "the call within the call" while travelling by train to the Loreto convent in Darjeeling from Calcutta for her annual retreat. "I was to leave the convent and help the poor while living among them. It was an order. To fail would have been to break the faith." One author later observed, "Though no one knew it at the time, Sister Teresa had just become *Mother* Teresa".

She began her missionary work with the poor in 1948, replacing her traditional Loreto habit with a simple white cotton *sari* decorated with a blue border. Mother Teresa adopted Indian citizenship, spent a few months in Patna to receive a basic medical training in the *Holy Family Hospital* and then ventured out into the slums.

Initially, she started a school in Motijhil (Calcutta); soon she started tending to the needs of the destitute and starving. In the beginning of 1949, she was joined in her effort by a group of young women and laid the foundations to create a new religious community helping the *"poorest among the poor"*.

Her efforts quickly caught the attention of Indian officials, including the prime minister, who expressed his appreciation.

Teresa wrote in her diary that her first year was fraught with difficulties. She had no income and had to resort to begging for food and supplies. Teresa experienced doubt, loneliness and the temptation to return to the comfort of convent life during these early months. She wrote in her diary:

Our Lord wants me to be a free nun covered with the poverty of the cross. Today, I learned a good lesson. The poverty of the poor must be so hard for them. While looking for a home I walked and walked till my arms and legs ached. I thought how much they must ache in body and soul, looking for a home, food and health. Then, the comfort of Loreto [her former congregation] came to tempt me. 'You have only to say the word and all that will be yours again,' the Tempter kept on saying... Of free choice, my God, and out of love for you, I desire to remain and do whatever be your Holy will in my regard. I did not let a single tear come.

4 *Mother Teresa*

Teresa received Vatican permission on 7 October 1950 to start the diocesan congregation that would become the Missionaries of Charity. Its mission was to care for, in her own words, "the hungry, the naked, the homeless, the crippled, the blind, the lepers, all those people who feel unwanted, unloved, uncared for throughout society, people that have become a burden to the society and are shunned by everyone."

It began as a small congregation with 13 members in Calcutta; by 1997 it had grown to more than 4,000 sisters running orphanages, AIDS hospices and charity centres worldwide, and caring for refugees, the blind, disabled, aged, alcoholics, the poor and homeless, and victims of floods, epidemics, and famine.

In 1952, Mother Teresa opened the first Home for the Dying in space made available by the city of Calcutta (Kolkata). With the help of Indian officials she converted an abandoned Hindu temple into the Kalighat Home for the Dying, a free hospice for the poor. She renamed it Kalighat, the Home of the Pure Heart (Nirmal Hriday). Those brought to the home received medical attention and were afforded the opportunity to die with dignity, according to the rituals of their faith; Muslims were read the Quran, Hindus received water from the Ganges, and Catholics received the Last Rites. "A beautiful death," she said, "is for people who lived like animals to die like angels—loved and wanted."

Mother Teresa soon opened a home for those suffering from Hansen's disease, commonly known as leprosy, and called the hospice Shanti Nagar (City of Peace). The Missionaries of Charity also established several leprosy outreach clinics throughout Calcutta, providing medication, bandages and food.

As the Missionaries of Charity took in increasing numbers of lost children, Mother Teresa felt the need to create a home for them. In 1955 she opened the Nirmala Shishu Bhavan, the Children's Home of the Immaculate Heart, as a haven for orphans and homeless youth.

The congregation soon began to attract both recruits and charitable donations, and by the 1960s had opened hospices, orphanages and leper houses all over India. Mother Teresa then expanded the congregation throughout the globe. Its first house

Biography 5

outside India opened in Venezuela in 1965 with five sisters. Others followed in Rome, Tanzania, and Austria in 1968; during the 1970s the congregation opened houses and foundations in dozens of countries in Asia, Africa, Europe and the United States. The Missionaries of Charity Brothers was founded in 1963, and a contemplative branch of the Sisters followed in 1976. Lay Catholics and non-Catholics were enrolled in the Co-Workers of Mother Teresa, the Sick and Suffering Co-Workers, and the Lay Missionaries of Charity. In answer to the requests of many priests, in 1981 Mother Teresa also began the Corpus Christi Movement for Priests, and in 1984 founded with Fr. Joseph Langford the Missionaries of Charity Fathers to combine the vocational aims of the Missionaries of Charity with the resources of the ministerial priesthood. By 2007 the Missionaries of Charity numbered approximately 450 brothers and 5,000 sisters worldwide, operating 600 missions, schools and shelters in 120 countries.

International Charity

Mother Teresa said "By blood, I am Albanian. By citizenship, an Indian. By faith, I am a Catholic nun. As to my calling, I belong to the world. As to my heart, I belong entirely to the Heart of Jesus."

In 1982, at the height of the Siege of Beirut, Mother Teresa rescued 37 children trapped in a front line hospital by brokering a temporary cease-fire between the Israeli army and Palestinian guerrillas. Accompanied by Red Cross workers, she travelled through the war zone to the devastated hospital to evacuate the young patients.

When Eastern Europe experienced increased openness in the late 1980s, she expanded her efforts to Communist countries that had previously rejected the Missionaries of Charity, embarking on dozens of projects. She was undeterred by criticism about her firm stand against abortion and divorce stating, "No matter who says what, you should accept it with a smile and do your own work." She visited the Soviet republic of Armenia following the 1988 earthquake, and met with Nikolai Ryzhkov, the Chairman of theCouncil of Ministers.

6 *Mother Teresa*

Mother Teresa travelled to assist and minister to the hungry in Ethiopia, radiation victims at Chernobyl, and earthquake victims in Armenia. In 1991, Mother Teresa returned for the first time to her homeland and opened a Missionaries of Charity Brothers home in Tirana, Albania.

By 1996, Mother Teresa was operating 517 missions in more than 100 countries. Over the years, Mother Teresa's Missionaries of Charity grew from twelve to thousands serving the "poorest of the poor" in 450 centres around the world. The first Missionaries of Charity home in the United States was established in the South Bronx, New York; by 1984 the congregation operated 19 establishments throughout the country. Mother Teresa was fluent in five languages: Bengali, Albanian, Serbian, English, and Hindi.

BEATIFICATION

For many, even in the Church, the Catholic practice of beatifying and canonizing is an enigma. Why does the Church do it? How does the Church do it? What are the implications of being canonized, or in the case of Mother Teresa of Calcutta, beatified?

First it should be noted that according to the testimony of Sacred Scripture every Christian is a saint. The Greek New Testament speaks in many places of the hagios (Acts 9:32; Rom 15:25, 31; Eph 1:1; Col. 1:2; Jude 1:3 and others). The Latin Vulgate speaks of the sancti, which is rendered in some English translations as the saints and in others as the holy ones.

As St. Peter tells Christians, "you are a chosen race, a royal priesthood, a holy nation, a people of his own, so that you may announce the praises of him who called you out of darkness into his wonderful light."

The saints are set apart by God through baptism, filled with His divine life (the Kingdom of God within), and called to announce that Kingdom's presence in the world to the whole human race. Thus it is that in the Scriptural usage all of those baptized into Christ and in the state of grace can rightly be called saints. In another sense, stricter and more technical, the saints are those in whom Christ's victory over sin, the devil and death has not just begun, as it has in us, but has been completed.

Biography 7

This is the case when the wayfaring state of earthy life is concluded and the holiness of life attained in the pilgrim's state is realized perfectly in heaven. Even while saying that no one is truly good but God (Mt 19:17), Christ called us to the perfection of goodness, of holiness, "be perfect as the heavenly Father is perfect" (Mt 5:48, Mt 19:21; Col. 4:12, James 1:4), since nothing imperfect will enter into heaven (Rev 21:27).

The early Church understood that only the Christian who followed Christ perfectly would go immediately into the heavenly Jerusalem. Others would enter the purifying fires of purgation "to be made perfect," from which they would not depart until they had "paid the last penny" (Mt 5:26, 1 Cor 3:13, 15). Since perfection was conformity to Christ in His death, a process begun at baptism, the martyr (literally, witness) for Christ was seen to have achieved the goal.

Thus, during the age of persecution (from Pentecost to 311 AD) esteem for those Christians who had been killed in hatred of the faith (in odium fidei) lead them to extol their example of heroic witness to Christ, to guard and preserve their relics (the trophies of victory over death) and to celebrate the anniversary of their birthday into eternal life. The Circular Letter of the Church of Smyrna on the Martyrdom of St. Polycarp (155 AD) illustrates this esteem perfectly.

We have at last gathered his bones, which are dearer to us than priceless gems and purer than gold, and laid them to rest where it was befitting they should lie.

And if it be possible for us to assemble again, may God grant us to celebrate the birthday of his martyrdom with gladness, thus to recall the memory of those who fought in the glorious combat, and to teach and strengthen by his example, those who shall come after us.

Finally, the greatest tribute of honor that could be rendered to the martyr was to have his or her name mentioned in the Canon (or Eucharistic Prayer) of the Mass, accompanying the Lord in His Redemptive Sacrifice. This was done on their feast day, the day of their entry into eternal life. The Roman Canon (Eucharistic Prayer 1) retains the eloquent testimony of the Roman Church for

8 *Mother Teresa*

the Mother of the Lord, for the apostles, and the most significant martyrs of Rome and Italy.

"In union with the whole Church...we honor Mary... Peter and Paul, Andrew, James, John, Thomas, Philip, Bartholomew, Matthew, Simon and Jude; we honor Linus, Cletus, Clement, Sixtus, Cornelius, Cyprian, Lawrence, Chrysogonus, John and Paul, Cosmas and Damian." (Communicantes)

"For ourselves, too, we ask some share in the fellowship of your apostles and martyrs, with John the Baptist, Stephen, Matthias, Barnabas, Ignatius, Alexander, Marcellinus, Peter, Felicity, Perpetua, Agatha, Lucy, Agnes, Cecilia, Anastasia and all the saints." (Nobis quoque peccatoribus)

Thus, in the early centuries of the Church the popular acclaim of sanctity in the martyrs, the veneration of their relics, the honoring of their names in private and liturgical prayer (with the consent of the local bishop) canonized important witnesses to Christ in the universal, and the local, Church, as examples of the perfect fidelity to which all Christians are called.

Although the age of martyrs has never truly ended, the relative peace that existed after the Edict of Milan in 311 meant that martyrdom was a rarer example of perfection than it had been. The Church began to look for other models of holiness, other ways in which conformity to Christ could be a witness to the faithful and the world, the living out in daily Christian life of the dying to self and living for Christ undertaken in baptism. This witness was found in those whose white martyrdom of heroic virtue confessed to the world the triumph of light over darkness, of grace over sin, of the new man over the old man (Eph 4:17-24), and thus of Christ over Satan. Thus, such Confessors, the witness of whose life had the fame of holiness, began to enter the roles of the canonized.

This cultus* (religious veneration) was generally of a single diocese, but as the fame of the person spread it could encompass several dioceses, and in the case of Mary, the apostles and other significant figures be universal in fact. Although the records of early Church Councils shows occasional interventions to correct abuses in the naming of saints and to establish criteria for their

Biography

acclamation, the process continued to be a local one with some few examples of Popes declaring saints of universal veneration.

The first canonical process seems to be that of Pope Urban II (1089-99), in the "Cause" of Nicholas of Trani. The Bishop of Trani was ordered to conduct a local investigation into his alleged sanctity and miracles, which then would be submitted to the Pope for judgement.

This first "Cause" dragged on over several pontificates, and seems not to have been concluded favorably. It also seems to have occasioned developments in the legal procedures themselves, Callistus II (1119-24) requiring all causes to include a critical biography of the Servant of God.

As often happens in the Church, abuses brought about major developments in Church practice. In 1170 Pope Alexander III decreed that no one could be declared a saint without the permission of the Supreme Pontiff. This was precipitated by the acclamation as saint of a Swedish "martyr" who was killed while drunk, and thus could not be truly said to be a willing witness for Christ. This regulation was formally incorporated into Church law by Pope Gregory IX in 1234.

The centralization of the canonization process in Rome was an inevitable development of the Church's theological and canonical Tradition. While the acclamation of the faithful and the acceptance of the bishop is in most cases an adequate witness to the holiness of the person, it only provides a moral certainty, a reasonable credibility, that the person is in heaven.

In order to give universal witness to the sanctity of someone a higher standard needed to be invoked, that of the charism of the infallibility of the Church. According to Catholic teaching the Church, the Mystical Christ, cannot err in matters of faith and morals (Jn 16:13).

The practical exercise of this infallibility falls to the apostolic office, which in the name and by the authority of Christ the Head of the Church intends to bind the faithful in a matter of faith or morals. This can be done either by the college of bishops as a whole, as in a Council (Acts 15:28 15:28), or by the Successor of

10 *Mother Teresa*

St. Peter (Lk 22:32, Acts 15:7-12 15:7-12). By the grace of the Holy Spirit Christ protects such judgements of universal import for the Church from error.

The common opinion of theologians historically, therefore, is that papal Canonization is an exercise of the charism of infallibility, protecting the Church from raising an unfitting individual to the universal veneration of the faithful. As in the case of a dogmatic declaration, the declaration of a saint inserts that person into the heart of the Church's life, in this case into the central mystery of the faith, the Eucharist, and must by its nature be free from error.

Cause for Beatification/Cause for Canonization.

According to an ancient theological axiom grace builds on nature. For this reason the Church is very careful to exhaust the human and reasonable means of determining the sanctity of a person before relying on supernatural ones. As noted earlier the papal canonization process quickly developed certain procedures whichh adt ob ef ollowedi nt hed iocesean di nR ome,s uchas t he collecting of evidence, of testimonies of witnesses and the writing of a critical biography.

By the fourteenth century two regular processes were in place, the Cause for Beatification and the Cause for Canonization. The first, when successfully concluded, allowed some measure of veneration of the Blessed by the faithful, in his or her diocese, by a religious order, by a nation.

The second permitted universal veneration of the Saint by the Church. The concluding stage of each was conducted in the form of a trial, with sides for or against. The office of the Promoter of the Faith or Devil's Advocate, who argued against the Servant of God, dates from this era.

The Processes have gone through several revisions and refinements over the centuries, including two recent ones, under Pope Paul VI in 1969 and under Pope John Paul II in 1983. Included in Pope Paul's reforms were the consolidation of the processes into a single Cause for Canonization. Notable in those of Pope John Paul II was the elimination of the Devil's Advocate, as well as many procedural changes.

Biography **11**

What it means to be Blessed.

Up until the beatification of a Servant of God Catholics must observe a strict rule of non cultus, meaning that while they may privately pray to and venerate an individual whom they believe to be in heaven there may not be any public acts of religious veneration. In fact, the presence of a cultus before the approval of the Church is given can end the candidacy of a Servant of God.

With Beatification a number of marks of veneration can be given to a person. The most important one is that a feast day, with its proper Mass and Office (Liturgy of the Hours), can be granted to particular dioceses and religious orders and congregations. For example, Blessed Takeri Tekawitha, the Lily of the Mohawks, is celebrated on the liturgical calendars of the U.S. and Canada. In the U.S. and Mexico there is a feast day for Blessed Juan Diego, the visionary of Guadalupe. By analogy, this privilege is somewhat akin to the practice of episcopal canonization earlier in Church history, except that a bishop manifests to Rome his flock's desire to venerate a Blessed and Rome grants such local veneration.

With beatification comes the restricted right to venerate the relics of Blessed Teresa, to have public prayers to them and to honor their images in places of worship where this is granted by the Holy See. It is restricted in the sense that it is the veneration of a part of the Church and not the whole, and lacks the finality of canonization.

Cultus. A certain negativity has attached itself to the English term cult (a false, exaggerated religious system) which should not be applied to the older, properly understood, Latin term cultus. The Latin term in the ancient world had the meaning of religious worship of God or a god. It could be applied to the True God (which would be legitimate) or to a pagan god among gods (which would be idolatry).

In using the term, but with specific theological meaning, the Church distinguishes between the forms of worship appropriate to God, Trinity, Christ and the Blessed Sacrament (called latria, worship or adoration, in the strict sense), and the forms of veneration and honor appropriate to the Blessed Virgin, the angels

12   *Mother Teresa*

and the saints (called hyperdulia or the greatest measure of veneration in the case of Mary and dulia or simple veneration in the case of the angels and other saints). It is a principle of justice that we must honor, respect and show gratitude in proper measure to those who are part of God's plan for our natural and supernatural life. God commands it in the Fourth Commandment.

This includes our natural parents who gave us life, but also those to whom we owe a debt for their role in the redemption (1 Cor 4:14-16, Heb. 13:7), first among whom is the Blessed Virgin Mary (Lk 1:48).But without the fidelity of the angels, who served as God's messengers, of the prophets, of the apostles, the evangelists, the Fathers and the great and holy men and women of all ages, we today would not have the faith.

That is the foundation of our individual and collective gratitude for the working of God's grace in their lives and thus of their cultus (in the way understood by the Church).

THE EARLY YEARS

"Keep the joy of loving the poor and share this joy with all you meet. Remember works of love are works of Peace. God Bless you." — Mother Teresa

Born Agnes Gonxha Bojaxhiu on August 26, 1910, in Skopje, Macedonia, in the former Yugoslavia, she was the youngest of three children. In her teens, Agnes became a member of a youth group in her local pairsh called Sodality. Through her involvement with their activities guided by a Jesuit priest, Agnes became interested in missionaries. At age 17, she responded to her first call of a vocation as a Catholic missionary nun. She joined an Irish order, the Sisters of Loretto, a community known for their missionary work in India. When she took her vows as a Sister of Loretto, she chose the name Teresa after Saint Thérèse of Lisieux.

In Calcutta, Sister Teresa taught geography and cathechism at St. Mary's High School. In 1944, she became the principal of St. Mary's. Soon Sister Teresa contracted tuberculosis, was unable to continue teaching and was sent to Darjeeling for rest and recuperation. It was on the train to Darjeeling that she received her second call -- "the call within the call". Mother Teresa recalled

Biography   13

later, "I was to leave the convent and work with the poor, living among them. It was an order. I knew where I belonged but I did not know how to get there."

In 1948, the Vatican granted Sister Teresa permission to leave the Sisters of Loretto and pursue her calling under the jurisdiction of the Archbishop of Calcutta.

Mother Teresa started with a school in the slums to teach the children of the poor. She also learned basic medicine and went into the homes of the sick to treat them. In 1949, some of her former pupils joined her. They found men, women, and children dying on the streets who were rejected by local hospitals. The group rented a room so they could care for helpless people otherwise condemned to die in the gutter. In 1950, the group was established by the Church as a Diocesan Congregation of the Calcutta Diocese. It was known as the Missionaries of Charity.

Leaving the Congregation of Our Lady of Loreto was the biggest sacrifice of my life," Mother Teresa told me. "I suffered a lot when I was 18, and left my family and country to go to the convent. But I suffered a lot more when I left the convent to begin the new experience that Jesus had proposed.

"I had received my spiritual formation, become a nun and consecrated my life to God in the Congregation of Our Lady of Loreto. I loved the work to which the congregation had assigned me at St. Mary's High School in Calcutta. For this reason, I paid a tremendous price by taking the step of leaving forever what had become my second family. When I closed the door of the convent behind me on Aug. 16, 1948, and found myself alone on the streets of Calcutta, I experienced a strong feeling of loss and almost of fear that was difficult to overcome."

The day before she left her convent, the Church had celebrated the feast of the Assumption, commemorating the Assumption into heaven, body and soul, of Mary, the mother of Jesus. The feast specifically exalts the ideals that Mother Teresa was striving to achieve in her new life.

Mary, bodily assumed into heaven, showed us Christians the importance of our bodies. The Church teaches that our bodies are

14 *Mother Teresa*

temples of the Holy Spirit, and that they will be gloriously resurrected. Jesus redeemed our bodies and souls by His passion and death. Mother Teresa was about to begin serving the poorest of the poor, people whose bodies often were appalling in appearance.

But even in these conditions, they were still children of God, whose bodies are destined to be resurrected. Mother Teresa wanted her last day in the convent to coincide with the feast of the Assumption as a way of giving deeper meaning to what she was about to do. She dedicated that day to prayer and meditation on the mission she was preparing to carry out, which would bring life and hope, as Mary's assumption into heaven did.

Thus, Mother Teresa left the convent on the morning of Aug. 16 for the first time in 18 years without her religious habit. She hardly made it to the middle of the street when she was overcome by anguish. Suddenly the reality of her new state in life became clear.

She was completely alone, with no house, no savings and no work. She did not know what she would eat and where she would sleep. She found herself in that same terrible condition of those who have nothing- those whom she wanted to serve.

She had to plan her own future. She was no longer part of a religious community, nor was she a layperson. She was still a nun, committed to God by vows of poverty, chastity and obedience. She had only obtained the Pope's permission to live temporarily outside the convent in order to found a new religious order.

She already had a very clear idea of what she wanted to do. The "command" that she received from Jesus was to "serve the poorest of the poor and to live among them and like them."

This tremendous ideal included unimaginable sacrifices. But it was an expression of total love, and for it, Mother Teresa made a revolutionary change in her life.

First she had to choose a habit that would reflect her lifestyle, and that of her future companions. She chose a simple white sari and sandals, which was the most common form of dress in India, and the color most often worn by the common people.

Biography **15**

The poor that she would be serving were mostly sick people, covered with sores and often smitten with leprosy. They urgently needed medical care, so she took a nursing course.

To do this, she moved to Patna, in the middle of the Ganges delta, where Mother Dengel and her Medical Missionary Sisters ran a hospital and offered nursing courses. "She was a good student," the sisters at Patna still remember. "She quickly learned in four months what is generally taught in a year."

Mother Teresa decided to live like the poor she would serve. The poor in Bengal ate rice and salt, so Mother Teresa tried to sustain herself for a while eating only a little rice seasoned with salt. However, such a diet did not provide enough nourishment. Mother Dengel's sisters intervened decisively. "If you continue to eat like that, in a short time you will waste away from consumption and die," she told her. "Then you won't be able to do anything for the poor."

Mother Teresa pondered their advice. She realized that she had been carried away by her enthusiasm and lack of experience and that her zeal could be fatal. She decided she and her future sisters would eat simply but sufficiently in order to remain in good health and totally dedicate themselves to serving the poor.

After four months, she returned to Calcutta to the only slum with which she was acquainted, located just behind St. Mary's High School. She had heard many horrible stories about the misery in this slum. While she was living at the convent, she had never wanted to step foot in this slum. Now she decided it would be her home.

She went there on Christmas Day, visited with the women and children, and searched for a place she could fix her living quarters. A woman rented a miserable shack for five rupees a month. This was her first house.

The next day, Mother Teresa's voice resounded in the shack, repeating the first letters of the Bengali alphabet. She had already found five children to teach. There was not even a table, chair, basin or chalkboard in her room, and she used a stick to trace the letters of the alphabet on the dirt floor.

16   *Mother Teresa*

A few months before, she had been the principal of the famous high school located just a few steps away and had taught the daughters of rich families. Now she was in a slum where people lived in misery among rats and cockroaches, teaching the children of people who were nobodies.

The heat was suffocating in her shack: 115 degrees with humidity surpassing 95 percent. Mother Teresa's clothing was clinging to her sweating body; she felt as though she was being invaded by filth. Everything was dirty: the shacks, the paths between the shacks that also served as sewer drains, the people and the rags they wore. On the floor of her shack she saw insects, rats and cockroaches. The children's heads were full of lice.

Mother Teresa remembered her school, her nice bed, the fans that ventilated the rooms, and the clean mosquito nets. She felt as though she had passed from heaven to hell. But it was there in that hell that the poor were living, the beloved brothers and sisters of Jesus, the people whom she wanted to serve. As Mother Teresa told me:

"The change was extremely difficult. In the convent I had lived without knowing what difficulties were. I had lacked nothing. Now everything was different. I slept where I happened to be, on the ground, often in hovels infested by rats. I ate what the people I was serving ate, and only when there was a little food.

"But I had chosen that lifestyle in order to literally live out the Gospel, especially where it says, 'I was hungry and you gave Me to eat, I was naked and you clothed Me, I was in prison and you came to find Me.' Among the poorest of the poor of Calcutta, I loved Jesus. When I love like that, I don't feel suffering or fatigue.

"On the other hand, after the very beginning, I didn't have time to get bored. The five children that I had gathered on the first day increased. Three days later there were 25, and by the end of the year there were 41.

"Through the children, I began to penetrate those labyrinths of the most squalid misery in Calcutta. At that time, the number of homeless in the city was about 1 million. I went from hut to hut, trying to be useful. I helped those who slept on the sides of

Biography 17

the street, who lived on garbage. I found the most atrocious suffering: the blind, the crippled, lepers, people with disfigured faces and deformed bodies, creatures who couldn't stand upright and who followed me on all fours asking for a little food.

"One day, in a heap of rubbish, I found a woman who was half dead. Her body had been bitten by rats and by ants. I took her to a hospital, but they told me that they didn't want her because they couldn't do anything for her. I protested and said that I wouldn't leave unless they hospitalized her. They had a long meeting and they finally granted my request. That woman was saved. Afterwards, when thanking me for what I had done for her, she said, 'And to think that it was my son who threw me in the garbage.'

"On another occasion, I absolutely needed to find a hut where I could shelter some people who had been abandoned. To find one, I walked for hours and hours under the scorching sun. By evening I felt as if I were going to faint from fatigue. Only then did I understand the degree of exhaustiont hatp oorp eopler each looking for a little food, a little medicine, or a roof for their heads.

"I gave my life completely to God, and He was the one who guided me. I felt His presence at every moment, and I saw His direct intervention.

One day, while I was walking along the streets of Calcutta, a priest came up to me, asking me to give a contribution for some worthy project. That morning I had left the house with all the money I had, five rupees, which amounted to about 30 cents. During the day, I had spent four on the poor. I had only one rupee to live on the next day and the following days if something didn't happen. Trusting in God, I gave my last rupee to that priest. In my mind I prayed, 'Lord, I don't have anything more, [but] I must think of You.'

"That evening a person whom I didn't know came to my shack. He gave me an envelope and said, 'This is for your work.' I was surprised because I had started my apostolate only a few days before and nobody knew me yet. I opened the envelope and found 50 rupees. At that moment, I felt as though God wanted

18   *Mother Teresa*

to give me a tangible sign of His approval for everything I was doing."

A VOCATION TO SERVICE

In 1952 the first Home for the Dying was opened in space made available by the City of Calcutta. Over the years, Mother Teresa's Missionaries of Charity grew from 12 to thousands serving the "poorest of the poor" in 450 centers around the world. Mother Teresa created many homes for the dying and the unwanted from Calcutta to New York to Albania. She was one of the pioneers of establishing homes for AIDS victims. For more than 45 years, Mother Teresa comforted the poor, the dying, and the unwanted around the world.

In 1966, the Missionaries of Charity Brothers was founded. Homes began to open in Rome, Tanzania, and Australia. In 1971, the first home in the United States was established in the South Bronx, New York.

Mother Teresa gained worldwide acclaim with her tireless efforts on behalf of world peace. Her work brought her numerous humanitarian awards, including : the Pope John XXIII Peace Prize and the Nobel Peace Prize in 1979. In receiving this award, Mother Teresa revolutionized the award ceremony. She insisted on a departure from the ceremonial banquet and asked that the funds, $6,000 be donated to the poor in Calcutta. This money would permit her to feed hundreds for a year.

She is stated to have said that earthly rewards were important only if they helped her help the world's needy.

Beginning in 1980, homes began to spring-up for drug addicts, prostitutes, battered women, and more orphanages and schools for poor children around the world. In 1985, Mother Teresa established the first hospice for AIDS victims in New York. Later homes were added in San Francisco and Atlanta. Mother Teresa was awarded Medal of Freedom, the highest U.S. civilian award.

In 1991, Mother Teresa returned for the first time to her native Albania and opened a home in Tirana. By this year, there were 168 homes established in India.

Biography 19

On February 3, 1994 at a National Prayer Breakfast, sponsored by the U.S. Senate and House of Representatives, in Washington, DC, Mother Teresa challenged the audience on such topics as family life and abortion. She said, "Please don't kill the child. I want the child. Give the child to me."

Mother Teresa traveled to help the hungry in Ethiopia, radiation victims at Chernobyl, and earthquake victims in Armenia. Her zeal and works of mercy knew no boundaries.

In November of 1996, Mother Teresa received the honorary U.S. citizenship.

MISSIONARIES OF CHARITY

On September 10, 1946, Teresa experienced what she later described as "the call within the call" while travelling to the Loreto convent in Darjeeling for her annual retreat. "I was to leave the convent and help the poor while living among them. It was an order. To fail would have been to break the faith." She began her missionary work with the poor in 1948, replacing her long, traditional Loreto habit with a simple white cotton sari decorated with a blue border and then venturing out into the slums." Initially she started a school in Motijhil; shortly thereafter, she started tending to the needs of the destitute and starving. Her efforts quickly caught the attention of Indian officials, including the Prime Minister, who expressed his appreciation.

Teresa wrote in her diary that her first year was fraught with difficulties. She had no income and had to resort to begging for food and supplies. Teresa experienced doubt, loneliness and the temptation to return to the comfort of convent life during these early months. She recorded in her diary: "Our Lord wants me to be a free nun covered with the poverty of the cross. Today I learned a good lesson. The poverty of the poor must be so hard for them. While looking for a home I walked and walked till my arms and legs ached. I thought how much they must ache in body and soul, looking for a home, food and health. Then the comfort of Loreto [her former order] came to tempt me. 'You have only to say the word and all that will be yours again,' the Tempter kept on saying... Of free choice, my God, and out of love for you, I

20 *Mother Teresa*

desire to remain and do whatever be your Holy will in my regard. I did not let a single tear come."

Teresa received Vatican permission on October 7, 1950 to start the diocesan congregation that would become the Missionaries of Charity. Its mission was to care for, in her own words, "the hungry, the naked, the homeless, the crippled, the blind, the lepers, all those people who feel unwanted, unloved, uncared for throughout society, people that have become a burden to the society and are shunned by everyone."

It began as a small order with 13 members in Calcutta; today it has more than 4,000 nuns running orphanages, AIDS hospices, and charity centres worldwide, and caring for refugees, the blind, disabled, aged, alcoholics, the poor and homeless, and victims of floods, epidemics, and famine.

In 1952 Mother Teresa opened the first Home for the Dying in space made available by the City of Calcutta. With the help of Indian officials she converted an abandoned Hindu temple into the Kalighat Home for the Dying, a free hospice for the poor. She renamed it Kalighat, the Home of the Pure Heart (Nirmal Hriday). Those brought to the home received medical attention and were afforded the opportunity to die with dignity, according to the rituals of their faith; Muslims were read the Quoran, Hindus received water from the Ganges, and Catholics received the Last Rites. "A beautiful death," she said, "is for people who lived like animals to die like angels-loved and wanted." She soon opened a home for those suffering from Hansen's disease, commonly known as leprosy, and called the hospice Shanti Nagar (City of Peace). The Missionaries of Charity also established several leprosy outreach clinics throughout Calcutta, providing medication, bandages and food.

As the Missionaries of Charity took in increasing numbers of lost children, Mother Teresa felt the need to create a home for them. In 1955 she opened the Nirmala Shishu Bhavan, the Children's Home of the Immaculate Heart, as a haven for orphans and homeless youth. The order soon began to attract both recruits and charitable donations, and by the 1960s had opened hospices, orphanages, and leper houses all over India.

Biography 21

Mother Teresa's order started to grow rapidly, with new homes opening throughout the globe. The order's first house outside India was in Venezuela, opened in 1965 with five sisters. Others followed in Rome, Tanzania, and Austria in 1968; during the 1970s the order would open houses and foundations in dozens of countries in Asia, Africa, Europe, and the United States.

Critics of Mother Teresa, most notably Christopher Hitchens, Tariq Ali and Aroup Chatterjee, have argued that her organization provided substandard care, was primarily interested in converting the dying to Catholicism, and used donations for missionary activities elsewhere, rather than being spent on improving the standard of health care. The Catholic Church has dismissed most of these criticisms.

DECLINING HEALTH AND DEATH

Mother Teresa suffered a heart attack in Rome in 1983 while visiting Pope John Paul II. After a second attack in 1989, she received an artificial pacemaker. In 1991, after a battle with pneumonia while in Mexico, she suffered further heart problems. She offered to resign her position as head of the Missionaries of Charity, but the sisters of the congregation, in a secret ballot, voted for her to stay. Mother Teresa agreed to continue her work as head of the congregation.

In April 1996, Mother Teresa fell and broke her collar bone. In August she suffered from malaria and failure of the left heart ventricle. She had heart surgery but it was clear that her health was declining. The Archbishop of Calcutta, Henry Sebastian D'Souza, said he ordered a priest to perform an exorcism on Mother Teresa with her permission when she was first hospitalised with cardiac problems because he thought she may be under attack by the devil.

On 13 March 1997, she stepped down from the head of Missionaries of Charity. She died on 5 September 1997.

At the time of her death, Mother Teresa's Missionaries of Charity had over 4,000 sisters, and an associated brotherhood of 300 members, operating 610 missions in 123 countries. These included hospices and homes for people with HIV/AIDS, leprosy

22   *Mother Teresa*

and tuberculosis, soup kitchens, children's and family counselling programs, personal helpers, orphanages, and schools. The Missionaries of Charity were also aided by Co-Workers, who numbered over 1 million by the 1990s.

Mother Teresa lay in repose in St Thomas, Kolkata for one week prior to her funeral, in September 1997. She was granted a state funeral by the Indian government in gratitude for her services to the poor of all religions in India. Her death was mourned in both secular and religious communities. In tribute, Nawaz Sharif, the Prime Minister of Pakistansaid that she was "a rare and unique individual who lived long for higher purposes. Her life-long devotion to the care of the poor, the sick, and the disadvantaged was one of the highest examples of service to our humanity." T he former U.N. Secretary-General Javier Pérez de Cuéllar said: "She is the United Nations. She is peace in the world."

RECOGNITION AND RECEPTION

In India

Mother Teresa had first been recognised by the Indian government more than a third of a century earlier when she was awarded the Padma Shri in 1962 and the Jawaharlal Nehru Award for International Understanding in 1969. She continued to receive major Indian awards in subsequent years, including India's highest civilian award, the Bharat Ratna, in 1980. Her official biography was written by an Indian civil servant, Navin Chawla, and published in 1992.

On 28 August 2010, to commemorate the 100th anniversary of her birth, the government of India issued a special 5 Rupee coin, being the sum she first arrived in India with. President Pratibha Patil said of Mother Teresa, "Clad in a white sari with a blue border, she and the sisters of Missionaries of Charity became a symbol of hope to many – the aged, the destitute, the unemployed, the diseased, the terminally ill, and those abandoned by their families.

Indian views on Mother Teresa were not uniformly favourable. Her critic Aroup Chatterjee, who was born and raised in Calcutta

Biography 23

but lived in London, reports that "she was not a significant entity in Calcutta in her lifetime". Chatterjee blames Mother Teresa for promoting a negative image of Calcutta, exaggerating the work done by her Mission, and misusing the funds and privileges at her disposal. Her presence and profile grated in parts of the Indian political world, as she often opposed the Hindu Right. The Bharatiya Janata Party clashed with her over the Christian Dalits, but praised her in death, sending a representative to her funeral. The Vishwa Hindu Parishad, on the other hand, opposed the government's decision to grant her a state funeral. Its secretary Giriraj Kishore said that "her first duty was to the Church and social service was incidental" and accused her of favouring Christians and conducting "secret baptisms" of the dying. But, in its front page tribute, the Indian fortnightly *Frontline* dismissed these charges as "patently false" and said that they had "made no impact on the public perception of her work, especially in Calcutta". Although praising her "selfless caring", energy and bravery, the author of the tribute was critical of Mother Teresa's public campaigning against abortion and that she claimed to be non-political when doing so.

In the Rest of the World

In 1962, Mother Teresa received the Philippines-based Ramon Magsaysay Award for International Understanding, given for work in South or East Asia. The citation said that "the Board of Trustees recognizes her merciful cognizance of the abject poor of a foreign land, in whose service she has led a new congregation". By the early 1970s, Mother Teresa had become an international celebrity. Her fame can be in large part attributed to the 1969 documentary *Something Beautiful for God*, which was filmed by Malcolm Muggeridge and his 1971 book of the same title. Muggeridge was undergoing a spiritual journey of his own at the time. During the filming of the documentary, footage taken in poor lighting conditions, particularly the Home for the Dying, was thought unlikely to be of usable quality by the crew. After returning from India, however, the footage was found to be extremely well lit. Muggeridge claimed this was a miracle of "divine light" from Mother Teresa herself. Others in the crew thought it was due to

24 *Mother Teresa*

a new type of ultra-sensitive Kodak film. Muggeridge later converted to Catholicism.

Around this time, the Catholic world began to honour Mother Teresa publicly. In 1971, Paul VI awarded her the first Pope John XXIIIPeace Prize, commending her for her work with the poor, display of Christian charity and efforts for peace. She later received thePacem in Terris Award (1976). Since her death, Mother Teresa has progressed rapidly along the steps towards sainthood, currently having reached the stage of having been beatified.

Mother Teresa was honoured by both governments and civilian organisations. She was appointed an honorary Companion of theOrder of Australiain 1982, "for service to the community of Australia and humanity at large." The United Kingdom and the United States each repeatedly granted awards, culminating in the Order of Merit in 1983, and honorary citizenship of the United States received on 16 November 1996. Mother Teresa's Albanian homeland granted her the Golden Honour of the Nation in 1994. Her acceptance of this and the Haitian Legion of Honour proved controversial. Mother Teresa attracted criticism from a number of people for implicitly giving support to the Duvaliersand to corrupt businessmen such as Charles Keating and Robert Maxwell. In Keating's case she wrote to the judge of his trial asking for clemency to be shown.

Universities in both the West and in India granted her honorary degrees. Other civilian awards include the Balzan Prize for promoting humanity, peace and brotherhood among peoples (1978), and the Albert Schweitzer International Prize (1975). In April of 1976, Mother Teresa visited the University of Scranton in northeasternPennsylvania where she was awarded the La Storta Medal for Human Service by the University's President Rev. William Byron, S.J. While there, she also addressed a crowd of 4,500 people. In her speech, she called the audience to "know poor people in your own home and local neighborhood," whether it meant feeding others or simply spreading joy and love. She continued, stating that "the poor will help us grow in sanctity, for they are Christ in the guise of distress," calling the students and residents of the city ofScrantonto give to suffering members in

Biography 25

their community. A gain, in August of 1987, Mother Teresa visited the University of Scranton and was awarded an honorary doctor of social science degree in recognition of her selfless service and her ministry to help the destitute and sick. She also spoke to the students as well as members of the Diocese of Scranton, numbering over 4000 individuals, telling them about her service to the "poorest of the poor" and instructing them to "do small things with great love."

In 1979, Mother Teresa was awarded theN obel Peace Prize, "for work undertaken in the struggle to overcome poverty and distress, which also constitutes a threat to peace." She refused the conventional ceremonial banquet given to laureates, and asked that the $192,000 funds be given to the poor in India, stating that earthly rewards were important only if they helped her help the world's needy. When Mother Teresa received the prize, she was asked, "What can we do to promote world peace?" She answered "Go home and love your family." Building on this theme in her Nobel Lecture, she said: "Around the world, not only in the poor countries, but I found the poverty of the West so much more difficult to remove. When I pick up a person from the street, hungry, I give him a plate of rice, a piece of bread, I have satisfied. I have removed that hunger. But a person that is shut out, that feels unwanted, unloved, terrified, the person that has been thrown out from society — that poverty is so hurtable [sic] and so much, and I find that very difficult." She also singled out abortion as "the greatest destroyer of peace today. Because if a mother can kill her own child - what is left for me to kill you and you kill me - there is nothing between."

During her lifetime, Mother Teresa was named 18 times in the yearly Gallup's most admired man and woman poll as one of the ten women around the world that Americans admired most, finishing first several times in the 1980s and 1990s. In 1999, a poll of Americans ranked her first in Gallup's List of Most Widely Admired People of the 20th Century. In that survey, she outpolled all other volunteered answers by a wide margin, and was in first place in all major demographic categories except the very young.

Criticism

After the award of the Nobel Peace Prize for 1979, Mother Teresa's adherence to the Church's condemnation of abortion and contraception attracted some negative attention in the Western media. Teresa was criticised for using her celebrity status to promote the Church's moral teachings on abortion and contraception.

The support, recognition, and donations she received also aroused criticism, particularly from atheists who were dismayed at what they considered to be people's gullibility. Some Bengali critics accused Mother Teresa of exploiting or even fabricating the degraded image of Calcutta to win international fame.

Allegations have been made that she knowingly accepted donations from disreputable sources. It was said that in one notorious case she knew or ought to have known that the money was stolen; and that she accepted money from the autocratic and corrupt Duvalier family in Haiti, which she visited in early 1981. In neither case were these allegations substantiated.

The increasing wealth of the order she founded became yet another grievance. On the one hand, large sums accumulated in checking (non-interest bearing) accounts in the United States, and large sums were being spent on opening new convents and increasing missionary work; on the other, her Home for the Dying continued to maintain the same austere ethos with which it had been founded, that is to say, as a place for those who had nowhere else to go – a point even hostile sources conceded.

She was also criticised for her view on suffering. She felt that suffering would bring people closer to Jesus. At a press conference during her October 1981 visit to Washington D.C, Mother Teresa stated, "I think it is very beautiful for the poor to accept their lot, to share it with the passion of Christ. I think the world is being much helped by the suffering of the poor people."

Critics complained that she did not apply donors' money on founding a modern medical facility in Calcutta, or transforming her Home for the Dying into a western-style hospice. Two writers in the Western medical press in the mid-1990's commented

Biography 27

adversely on an approach to illness and suffering that disregarded elements of modern medical care, such as systematic diagnosis and strong analgesics. Her defenders pointed out that the Home did not claim to offer primary medical care, but was a refuge for the dying, with nowhere else to go. Apart from the barriers that advanced technologies and the need for specialist physicians to manage pain would interpose between carers and those they cared for (disrupting the ethos of the Home), the use of opioids in India for managing cancer pain remains — ten years after Mother Teresa's death — highly problematic for legal, regulatory, cultural, and other reasons (including supply interruptions, harsh punishments imposed for even minor infractions of the rules, and the fear of addiction by health workers). Despite the lack of sophisticated analgesic regimes, volunteers (including those with western medical qualifications and experience) reported that her Home for the Dying was a place of joy not sadness. As late as 2001, researchers could write that "pain relief is a new notion in [India]", and "palliative care training has been available only since 1997". It was only in 2012 that the government of West Bengal finally amended the applicable regulations simplifying "the process of possession, transport, purchase, sale and import of inter-state of morphine or any preparation containing morphine by 'Recognized Medical Institution'."

Notwithstanding these practical considerations, the advanced treatment Mother Teresa received for an increasingly aggravated heart condition (which eventually killed her) was said to evidence her personal hypocrisy, while the factors that impelled the Missionaries of Charity to prolong her active life were ignored. She herself — at an advanced age — attempted to resign as Superior generalo f the order, but the sisters were unanimous in re-electing her in 1990, when she was already 80 years old.

On February 2015, Mohan Bhagwat, leader of the Hindu right-wing organisation RSS said that her objective was "to convert the person, who was being served, into a Christian" Former RSS spokesperson MG Vaidhya backed Bhagwat's remarks. The party accused the media of "distorting facts about Bhagwat's remarks". Trinamool Congress MP Derek O'Brien, CPI leader Atul

28 *Mother Teresa*

Anjan protested against the comments and Delhi's chief minister Arvind Kejriwal said "I worked with Mother Teresa for a few months at Nirmal Hriday ashram in Kolkata. She was a noble soul. Please spare her."

SPIRITUAL LIFE

Analyzing her deeds and achievements, John Paul II asked: "Where did Mother Teresa find the strength and perseverance to place herself completely at the service of others? She found it in prayer and in the silent contemplation of Jesus Christ, his Holy Face, his Sacred Heart." Privately, Mother Teresa experienced doubts and struggles over her religious beliefs which lasted nearly 50 years until the end of her life, during which "she felt no presence of God whatsoever", "neither in her heart or in the eucharist" as put by her postulator Rev. Brian Kolodiejchuk. Mother Teresa expressed grave doubts about God's existence and pain over her lack of faith:

Where is my faith? Even deep down... there is nothing but emptiness and darkness... If there be God—please forgive me. When I try to raise my thoughts to Heaven, there is such convicting emptiness that those very thoughts return like sharp knives and hurt my very soul... How painful is this unknown pain—I have no Faith. Repulsed, empty, no faith, no love, no zeal,... What do I labor for? If there be no God, there can be no soul. If there be no soul then, Jesus, You also are not true.

With reference to the above words, the Rev. Brian Kolodiejchuk, her postulator (the official responsible for gathering the evidence for her sanctification) said he thought that some might misinterpret her meaning, but her faith that God was working through her remained undiminished, and that while she pined for the lost sentiment of closeness with God, she did not question his existence. and that she may have experienced something similar to what is believed of Jesus Christ when crucified who was heard to say "Eli Eli lama sabachthani?" which is translated to "My God, My God, why have you forsaken me?" Brian Kolodiejchuk, drew comparisons to the 16th century mystic St. John of the Cross, who coined the term the "Dark Night of the Soul". Many other saints

Biography 29

had similar experiences ofspiritual dryness, or what Catholics believe to be spiritual tests ("passive purifications"), such as Mother Teresa's namesake, St. Therese of Lisieux, who called it a "night of nothingness." Contrary to the mistaken belief by some that the doubts she expressed would be an impediment to canonisation, just the opposite is true; it is very consistent with the experience of canonised mystics.

Mother Teresa described, after ten years of doubt, a short periodo fr enewedf aith.A tt het imeo ft hed eatho fPo pePi usX II in the fall of 1958, praying for him at a requiem mass, she said she had been relieved of "the long darkness: that strange suffering." However, five weeks later, she described returning to her difficulties in believing.

Mother Teresa wrote many letters to her confessors and superiors over a 66-year period. She had asked that her letters be destroyed,c oncernedt hat"p eoplew illt hinkm oreo fm e—lesso f Jesus." However, despite this request, the correspondences have been compiled in *Mother Teresa: Come Be My Light* (Doubleday). In one publicly released letter to a spiritual confidant, the Rev. Michael van der Peet, she wrote, "Jesus has a very special love for you. [But] as for me, the silence and the emptiness is so great, that I look and do not see, — Listen and do not hear — the tongue moves [in prayer] but does not speak... I want you to pray for me — that I let Him have [a] free hand."

In his first encyclical *Deus caritas est*, Benedict XVI mentioned Teresa of Calcutta three times and he also used her life to clarify one of his main points of the encyclical. "In the example of Blessed Teresa of Calcutta we have a clear illustration of the fact that time devoted to God in prayer not only does not detract from effective and loving service to our neighbour but is in fact the inexhaustible source of that service." Mother Teresa specified that "It is only by mental prayer and spiritual reading that we can cultivate the gift of prayer."

Although there was no direct connection between Mother Teresa's order and the Franciscan orders, she was known as a great admirer of St. Francis of Assisi. A ccordingly, her influence and life show influences of Franciscan spirituality. The Sisters of

30 *Mother Teresa*

Charity recite the peace prayer of St. Francis every morning during thanksgiving after Communionand many of the vows and emphasis of her ministry are similar. St. Francis emphasised poverty, chastity, obedience and submission to Christ. He also devoted much of his own life to service of the poor, especially lepers in the area where he lived.

MIRACLE AND BEATIFICATION

After Mother Teresa's death in 1997, the Holy See began the process of beatification, the third step toward possible canonisation. This process requires the documentation of amiracle performed from the intercession of Mother Teresa.

In 2002, the Vatican recognised as a miracle the healing of a tumor in the abdomen of an Indian woman, Monica Besra, after the application of a locket containing Mother Teresa's picture. Besra said that a beam of light emanated from the picture, curing the cancerous tumor. Critics — including some of Besra's medical staff and, initially, Besra's husband — said that conventional medical treatment had eradicated the tumor. Dr. Ranjan Mustafi, who told *The New York Times* he had treated Besra, said that the cyst was not cancer at all but a cyst caused by tuberculosis. He said, "It was not a miracle.... She took medicines for nine months to one year." According to Besra's husband, "My wife was cured by the doctors and not by any miracle."

An opposing perspective of the claim is that Besra's medical records contain sonograms, prescriptions, and physicians' notes that could prove whether the cure was a miracle or not. Besra has claimed that Sister Betta of the Missionaries of Charity is holding them. *Time*m agazine received a "no comments" statement from Sister Betta. The officials at the Balurghat Hospital where Besra was seeking medical treatment have claimed that they are being pressured by the Catholic order to declare the cure a miracle.

In the process of examining Teresa's suitability for beatification and canonisation, the Roman Curia (the Vatican) pored over a great deal of documentation of published and unpublished criticism of her life and work. Concerning allegations raised by journalist Christopher Hitchens, Vatican officials have responded

Biography

by saying that these have been investigated by the agency charged with such matters, the Congregation for the Causes of Saints, and that they found no obstacle to Mother Teresa's beatification. Because of the attacks she has received, some Catholic writers have called her a sign of contradiction. The beatification of Mother Teresa took place on 19 October 2003, thereby bestowing on her the title "Blessed." A second miracle is required for her to proceed to canonisation.

FACTS ABOUT MOTHER TERESA

Mother Teresa is a household name for her good works, but many people don't know much about her beyond "nun who helped the poor." On the anniversary of her being awarded the Nobel Peace Prize, here are 20 facts about Mother Teresa.

1. Agnes Gonxha Bojaxhiu was born Aug. 26, 1910, in Macedonia to a financially comfortable Albanian family (they owned two houses, one of which they lived in). Her father died when she was 8, ending her family's financial security.

2. Agnes was fascinated with missionaries from an early age, and by 12 she knew that she would commit herself to a religious vocation.

3. When she was 18, Agnes left home and joined the Sisters of Loreto in Rathfarnham, Ireland.

4. Although she lived to be 87, she never saw her mother or sister again after the day she left for Ireland.

5. After a year learning English in Ireland, Agnes transferred to the Sisters of Loreto convent in Darjeeling, India.

6. She took her vows as a nun in 1931, choosing the name Teresa to honor Saints Therese of Lisieux and Teresa of Avila.

7. Therese of Lisieux, the patron saint of Australia, is also the patron of missionaries, florists and AIDS sufferers, among others. Spain's patron saint, Teresa of Avila, is also the patron of religious orders and lacemakers.

8. Sister Teresa began teaching history and geography in Calcutta at St. Mary's, a high school for the daughters of

32   *Mother Teresa*

the wealthy. She remained there for 15 years and enjoyed the work, but was distressed by the poverty she saw all around her.

9. In 1946 Teresa traveled to Darjeeling for a retreat. It was on that journey that she realized what her true calling was: "I heard the call to give up all and follow Christ into the slums to serve him among the poorest of the poor."

10. It took two years of preparation before she was able to begin doing the work she felt compelled to do. She needed to receive permission from the Sisters of Loreto to leave the order – while retaining her vows – as well as permission from the Archbishop of Calcutta to live and work among the poor. She also prepared by taking a nursing course.

11. In 1948 Sister Teresa set aside her nun's habit – adopting instead the simple sari and sandals worn by the women she would be living among – and moved to a small rented hovel in the slums to begin her work.

12. Teresa's first year in the slums was particularly hard. She was used to a life of comparative comfort, and now she had no income and no way to obtain food and supplies other than begging. She was often tempted to return to convent life, and had to rely on her determination and faith to get herself through it.

13. One of her first projects was to teach the children of the poor – drawing on her experience with teaching the children of the rich. She didn't have any equipment or supplies this time, but she taught them to read and write by writing in the dirt with sticks.

14. In addition to promoting literacy, Teresa taught the children basic hygiene. She visited their families, inquiring about their needs and helping provide for them when she could.

15. Word began to spread about Mother Teresa's good works, and soon she had other volunteers wanting to help. By 1950 she was able to start the Mission of Charity – a congregation dedicated to caring for "the hungry, the naked, the homeless, the crippled, the blind, the lepers, all those people who feel unwanted, unloved, uncared for

Biography

33

throughout society, people that have become a burden to the society and are shunned by everyone."

16. She went on to open a hospice for the poor, a home for sufferers of leprosy, and a home for orphans and homeless youths.

17. Mother Teresa was honored with many awards throughout her life, from the Indian Padma Shri in 1962 to the inaugural Pope John XXIII Peace Prize in 1971 to Albania's Golden Honour of the Nation in 1994... and, most famously, the Nobel Peace Prize in 1979.

18. She refused the traditional Nobel honor banquet, instead requesting that the $192,000 budget be given to help the poor of India.

19. She continued her work with the poor for the rest of her life, leading the Missionaries of Charity until just months before her death Sept. 5, 1997.

20. The Catholic Church has begun to move Mother Teresa along the steps toward sainthood, and she was beatified in 2003. Her official title is now Blessed Teresa of Calcutta.

LEGACY AND DEPICTIONS IN POPULAR CULTURE

Commemoration

Mother Teresa inspired a variety of commemorations. She has been memorialised through museums, been named patroness of various churches, and had various structures and roads named after her, including Albania's international airport. Mother Teresa Day *(Dita e Nënë Terezës)* on 19 October is a public holiday in Albania. In 2009 the Memorial House of Mother Teresa was opened in her hometown Skopje, in Macedonia. The Roman Catholic cathedral in Pristina is also dedicated in her honour. Its construction sparked controversy in Muslim circles in 2011; local Muslim leaders claimed that the cathedral was too large for Pristina's small Catholic community and complained that most Muslim places of worship in the city were far smaller. An initiative to erect a monument to Mother Teresa in the town of Peæ that same year was also protested

34

by some Albanian Muslims. A youth group calling itself the Muslim Youth Forum started a petition demanding that a monument to Albanian veterans of the Kosovo War be erected instead, and collected some 2,000 signatures by May 2011. The Muslim Youth Forum claimed that the building of a Mother Teresa monument would represent an insult to the town's Muslim community, which makes up about 98 percent of the population. Noli Zhita, the group's spokesperson, claimed that Mother Teresa was not an Albanian but a Vlach from Macedonia. He described the monument's planned construction as part of a plot to "Christianize" Kosovo. The Mayor of Peæ, Ali Berisha, voiced support for the monument's construction and indicated that the head of the Islamic community in the town had not raised any objections.

Mother Teresa Women's University, Kodaikanal, Tamil Nadu, has been established in 1984 as a public university by government of Tamil Nadu, India.

Mother Theresa Post Graduate and Research Institute of Health Sciences, Pondicherry has been established in 1999 by Government of Puducherry, India.

The charitable organisation Sevalaya runs the Mother Teresa Girls Home, named in her honour and designed to provide poor and orphan girls children in the vicinity of the underserved Kasuva village in Tamil Nadu with free food, clothing, shelter, and education.

Film and literature

Mother Teresa is the subject of the 1969 documentary film and 1972 book *Something Beautiful for God*, a 1997 Art Film Festival award winning film starring Geraldine Chaplincalled *Mother Teresa: In the Name of God's Poor*, a 2003 Italian miniseries titled *Mother Teresa of Calcutta*, (which was re-released in 2007 and received a CAMIE award,) and was portrayed by Megan Fox in a satirical film-within-a-film in the 2007 movie *How to Lose Friends & Alienate People*. Hitchens' 1994 documentary about her, *Hell's Angel*, claims that she urged the poor to accept their fate, while the rich are portrayed as being favoured by God.

2 Early Life of Mother Teresa

"Keep the joy of loving the poor and share this joy with all you meet. Remember works of love are works of Peace. God Bless you."

- Mother Teresa

Born Agnes Gonxha Bojaxhiu on August 26, 1910, in Skopje, Macedonia, in the former Yugoslavia, she was the youngest of three children. In her teens, Agnes became a member of a youth group in her local pairsh called Sodality. Through her involvement with their activities guided by a Jesuit priest, Agnes became interested in missionaries. At age 17, she responded to her first call of a vocation as a Catholic missionary nun. She joined an Irish order, the Sisters of Loretto, a community known for their missionary work in India. When she took her vows as a Sister of Loretto, she chose the name Teresa after Saint Thérèse of Lisieux.

CHILDHOOD & EARL Y LIFE

- Born to Nikolle and Dranafile Bojaxhiu in Skopje, Mother Teresa was the youngest child of the Albanian couple. She was born on August 26, 1919 and was baptized the following day as Agnes Gonxhe Bojaxhiu, a date she considered her 'true birthday'. She received her First Communion when she was five and a half.

- Raised in a devoutly Catholic family, her father was an entrepreneur by profession. Her mother had a spiritual and religious bent of mind and was active participant in the local church activities.

- Sudden and tragic death of her father when she was eight years old left young Agnes disheartened. Despite facing financial crisis, Dranafile did not compromise on the upbringing of her children and raised them with utmost love, care and affection. Over the years, young Agnes grew extremely close to her mother.

36 *Mother Teresa*

- It was Dranafile's firm belief and religious attitude that greatly influenced Agnes character and future vocation. A pious and compassionate woman, she instilled in Agnes a deep commitment to charity, which was further affirmed by her involvement in the Jesuit parish of the Sacred Heart.

Religious Calling

- As Agnes turned 18, she found her true calling as a nun and left home for good to enrol herself at the Institute of the Blessed Mary Virgin, also called Sisters of Loreto, in Ireland. It was there that she first received the name Sister Mary Teresa after St Therese of Lisieux.
- After a year of training, Sister Mary Teresa came to India in 1929 and initiated her novitiate in Darjeeling, West Bengal, as a teacher at St Teresa's School. She learned the local language of the state, Bengali.
- Sister Teresa took her first religious vows in May 1931. Thereafter, she was assigned duty at the Loreto Entally community of Calcutta and taught at St Mary's School.
- Six years later, on May 24, 1937, she took her Final Profession of Vows and with that acquired the name, which the world recognizes her with today, Mother Teresa. The next twenty years of her life, Mother Teresa dedicated to serving as a teacher at the St Mary's School, graduating to the post of the principal in 1944.
- Within the walls of the convent, Mother Teresa was known for her love, kindness, compassion and generosity. Her unflinching commitment to serving the society and mankind was greatly recognized by students and teachers. However, just as much Mother Teresa enjoyed teaching young girls, she was greatly disturbed by the poverty and misery that was prevalent in Calcutta.

SYNOPSIS

Baptized on August 27, 1910, in Skopje, Macedonia, Mother Teresa taught in India for 17 years before she experienced her 1946 "call within a call" to devote herself to caring for the sick and poor.

Early Life of Mother T eresa 37

Her order established a hospice; centers for the blind, aged, and disabled; and a leper colony. She was summoned to Rome in 1968, and in 1979 received the Nobel Peace Prize for her humanitarian work.

EARLY LIFE

Catholic nun and missionary Mother Teresa was born circa August 26, 1910 (her date of birth is disputed), in Skopje, the current capital of the Republic of Macedonia. On August 27, 1910, a date frequently cited as her birthday, she was baptized as Agnes Gonxha Bojaxhiu. Mother Teresa's parents, Nikola and Dranafile Bojaxhiu, were of Albanian descent; her father was an entrepreneur who worked as a construction contractor and aTRADER of medicines and other goods. The Bojaxhius were a devoutly Catholic family, and Nikola Bojaxhiu was deeply involved in the local church as well as in city politics as a vocal proponent of Albanian independence.

In 1919, when Mother Teresa was only 8 years old, her father suddenly fell ill and died. While the cause of his death remains unknown, many have speculated that political enemies poisoned him. In the aftermath of her father's death, Mother Teresa became extraordinarily close to her mother, a pious and compassionate woman who instilled in her daughter a deep commitment to charity.

Although by no means wealthy, Drana Bojaxhiu extended an open invitation to the city's destitute to dine with her family. "My child, never eat a single mouthful unless you are sharing it with others," she counseled her daughter. When Mother Teresa asked who the people eating with them were, her mother uniformly responded, "Some of them are our relations, but all of them are our people."

Religious Calling

Mother Teresa attended a convent-run primary school and then a state-run secondary school. As a girl, Mother Teresa sang in the local Sacred Heart choir and was often asked to sing solos. The congregation made an annual pilgrimage to the chapel of the

38

Mother Teresa

Madonna of Letnice atop Black Mountain in Skopje, and it was on one such trip at the age of 12 that Mother Teresa first felt a calling to a religious life. Six years later, in 1928, an 18-year-old Agnes Bojaxhiu decided to become a nun and set off for Ireland to join the Loreto Sisters of Dublin. It was there that she took the name Sister Mary Teresa after Saint Thérèse of Lisieux.

A year later, Mother Teresa traveled on to Darjeeling, India for the novitiate period; in May 1931, Mother Teresa made her First Profession of Vows. Afterward she was sent to Calcutta, where she was assigned to teach at Saint Mary's High School for Girls, a school run by the Loreto Sisters and dedicated to teaching girls from the city's poorest Bengali families. Mother Teresa learned to speak both Bengali and Hindi fluently as she taught geography and history and dedicated herself to alleviating the girls' poverty through education.

On May 24, 1937, she took her Final Profession of Vows to a life of poverty, chastity and obedience. As was the custom for Loreto nuns, she took on the title of "mother" upon making her final vows and thus became known as Mother Teresa. Mother Teresa continued to teach at Saint Mary's, and in 1944 she became the school's principal. Through her kindness, generosity and unfailing commitment to her students' education, she sought to lead them to a life of devotion to Christ. "Give me the strength to be ever the light of their lives, so that I may lead them at last to you," she wrote in prayer.

A New Calling

However, on September 10, 1946, Mother Teresa experienced a second calling that would forever transform her life. She was riding a train from Calcutta to the Himalayan foothills for a retreat when Christ spoke to her and told her to abandon teaching to work in the slums of Calcutta aiding the city's poorest and sickest people. "I want Indian Nuns, Missionaries of Charity, who would be my fire of love amongst the poor, the sick, the dying and the little children," she heard Christ say to her on the train that day. "You are I know the most incapable person — weak and sinful but

Early Life of Mother Teresa

just because you are that—I want to use You for My glory. Wilt thou refuse?"

Since Mother Teresa had taken a vow of obedience, she could not leave her convent without official permission. After nearly a year and a half of lobbying, in January 1948 she finally received approval from the local Archbishop Ferdinand Périer to pursue this new calling.

That August, wearing the blue and white sari that she would always wear in public for the rest of her life, she left the Loreto convent and wandered out into the city. After six months of basic medical training, she voyaged for the first time into Calcutta's slums with no more specific goal than to aid "the unwanted, the unloved, the uncared for."

The Missionaries of Charity

Mother Teresa quickly translated this somewhat vague calling into concrete actions to help the city's poor. She began an open-air school and established a home for the dying destitute in a dilapidated building she convinced the city government to donate to her cause. In October 1950, she won canonical recognition for a new congregation, the Missionaries of Charity, which she founded with only 12 members—most of them former teachers or pupils from St. Mary's School.

As the ranks of her congregation swelled and donations poured in from around India and across the globe, the scope of Mother Teresa's charitable activities expanded exponentially. Over the course of the 1950s and 1960s, she established a leper colony, an orphanage,an ursingh ome,af amilyc linican das tringo fm obile health clinics.

In 1971, Mother Teresa traveled to New York City to open her first American-based house of charity, and in the summer of 1982, she secretly went to Beirut, Lebanon, where she crossed between Christian East Beirut and Muslim West Beirut to aid children of both faiths. In 1985, Mother Teresa returned to New York and spoke at the 40th anniversary of the United Nations General Assembly. While there, she also opened Gift of Love, a home to care for those infected with HIV/AIDS.

International Charity and Recognition

In February 1965, Pope Paul VI bestowed the Decree of Praise upon the Missionaries of Charity, which prompted Mother Teresa to begin expanding internationally. By the time of her death in 1997, the Missionaries of Charity numbered over 4,000 — in addition to thousands more lay volunteers — with 610 foundations in 123 countries on all seven continents.

The Decree of Praise was just the beginning, as Mother Teresa received various honors for her tireless and effective charity. She was awarded the Jewel of India, the highest honor bestowed on Indian civilians, as well as the now-defunct Soviet Union'sGOLDM edal of the Soviet Peace Committee. And in 1979, Mother Teresa won her highest honor when she was awarded the Nobel Peace Prize in recognition of her work "in bringing help to suffering humanity."

Controversy

Despite this widespread praise, Mother Teresa's life and work have not gone without criticism. In particular, she has drawn criticism for her vocal endorsement of some of the Catholic Church's more controversial doctrines, such as opposition to contraception and abortion. "I feel the greatest destroyer of peace today is abortion," Mother Teresa said in her 1979 Nobel lecture.

In 1995, she publicly advocated a "no" vote in the Irish referendum to end the country's constitutional ban on divorce and remarriage. The most scathing criticism of Mother Teresa can be found in Christopher Hitchens' book *The Missionary Position: Mother Teresa in Theory and Practice*, in which Hitchens argued that Mother Teresa glorified poverty for her own ends and provided a justification for the preservation of institutions and beliefs that sustained widespread poverty.

Death and Legacy

After several years of deteriorating health in which she suffered from heart, lung and kidney problems, Mother Teresa died on September 5, 1997 at the age of 87. Since her death, Mother Teresa has remained in the public spotlight. In particular, the publication

Early Life of Mother T eresa   **41**

of her private correspondence in 2003 caused aWHOLESALE re-evaluation of her life by revealing the crisis of faith she suffered for most of the last 50 years of her life.

In one despairing letter to a confidant, she wrote, "Where is my Faith—even deep down right in there is nothing, but emptiness & darkness—My God—how painful is this unknown pain—I have no Faith—I dare not utter the words & thoughts that crowd in my heart — & make me suffer untold agony." While such revelations are shocking considering her public image of perfect faith, they have also made Mother Teresa a more relatable and human figure to all those who experience doubt in their beliefs.

For her unwavering commitment to aiding those most in need, Mother Teresa stands out as one of the greatest humanitarians of the 20th century. She combined profound empathy and a fervent commitment to her cause with incredible organizational and managerial skills that allowed her to develop a vast and effective international organization of missionaries to help impoverished citizens all across the globe.

SISTER TERESA IN CALCUTT A

In Calcutta, Sister Teresa taught geography and cathechism at St. Mary's High School. In 1944, she became the principal of St. Mary's. Soon Sister Teresa contracted tuberculosis, was unable to continue teaching and was sent to Darjeeling for rest and recuperation. It was on the train to Darjeeling that she received her second call — "the call within the call". Mother Teresa recalled later, "I was to leave the convent and work with the poor, living among them. It was an order. I knew where I belonged but I did not know how to get there."

In 1948, the Vatican granted Sister Teresa permission to leave the Sisters of Loretto and pursue her calling under the jurisdiction of the Archbishop of Calcutta.

Call Within a Call

- Little did she know that the journey from Calcutta to Darjeeling made by Mother Teresa for her yearly retreat, on September 10, 1946 would transform her life completely.

- She experienced a call within a call - a call from the Almighty to fulfil His heartfelt desire of serving the 'poorest of the poor'. Mother Teresa explained the experience as an order from Him, which she could not fail on any condition as it would mean breaking the faith.

- He asked Mother Teresa to establish a new religious community,M issionarieso fC harityS isters,w hichw ould be dedicated to serving the 'poorest of the poor'. The community would work in the slums of Calcutta and help the poorest and sick people.

- Since Mother Teresa had taken a vow of obedience, leaving the convent without official permission was impossible. For nearly two years, she lobbied for initiating the new religious community, which brought favourable result in the January of 1948 as she received a final approval from the local Archbishop Ferdinand Périer to pursue the new calling.

- On August 17, 1948, clad in a white blue-bordered saree, Mother Teresa walked past the gate of the convent, which had been her habitat for almost two decades, to enter the world of poor, a world that needed her, a world which He wanted her to serve, a world she knew of as her own!

- Gaining Indian citizenship, Mother Teresa travelled all the way to Patna, Bihar to gain medical training at the Medical Mission Sisters. After completing her short course, Mother Teresa returned to Calcutta and found her temporary lodging at Little Sisters of the Poor.

- Her first outing was on December 21, 1948 to help the people in the slums. Her main mission was to serve Him by helping the 'unwanted, unloved, and uncared'. From then on, Mother Teresa reached out to the poor and needy each day, fulfilling His desire to radiate love, kindness and compassion.

- Starting off all alone, Mother Teresa was soon joined by voluntary helpers, most of which were former students and teachers, who accompanied her in her mission to fulfil His vision. With time, financial help also came in.

Early Life of Mother Teresa

- Mother Teresa then started an open air school and soon established a home for the dying and destitute in a dilapidated home, which she convinced the government to donate to her.
- October 7, 1950 was historic day in the life of Mother Teresa; she finally received permission by the Vatican to start the congregation that eventually came to be known as Missionaries of Charity.
- Starting off with merely 13 members, the Missionaries of Charity went on to become one of the most significant and recognized congregations in the world. As the ranks of congregation raised and financial aid came in easily, Mother Teresa expanded her scope for charitable activities exponentially.
- In 1952, she inaugurated the first Home for the Dying, where people brought to this home received medical help and accorded the opportunity to die with dignity. Adhering to the different faith that people came in from, all who died were given their last ceremonies according to the religion they followed, thus dying a death of dignity.
- The next step was initiating a home for those suffering from Hansen's disease, commonly known as leprosy. The home was called Shanti Nagar. Additionally, several clinics were formed in the city of Calcutta which provided medication, bandage and food to those suffering from leprosy.
- In 1955, Mother Teresa opened a home for the orphans and homeless youths. She named it as Nirmala Shishu Bhavan, or the Children's Home of the Immaculate Heart.
- What started as a small effort soon grew in size and number, attracting recruits and financial help. By 1960, Missionaries of Charity had opened several hospices, orphanages and leper houses all over India.
- Meanwhile, in 1963, Missionaries of Charity Brothers was founded. The main aim behind the inauguration of Missionaries of Charity Brother was to better respond to the physical and spiritual needs of the poor.

- Furthermore, in 1976, a contemplative branch of the sisters was opened. Two years later, a contemplative brothers' branch was inaugurated. In 1981, she began the Corpus Christi Movement for Priests and in 1984 the Missionaries of Charity Fathers was initiated. The initiation of the same was to combine the vocational aim of Missionaries of charity with the resource of ministerial priesthood.
- Mother Teresa, then, formed the Co-Workers of Mother Teresa, the Sick and Suffering Co-Workers, and the Lay Missionaries of Charity.
- The congregation, which was limited to India, opened its first house outside India in Venezuela in 1965 with five sisters. However, this was just the beginning, as many more houses came up in Rome, Tanzania and Austria. By 1970s, the order had reached several countries in Asia, Africa, Europe and United States.
- In 1982, Mother Teresa rescued almost 37 children who were trapped in a front line hospital in Beirut. With the help of a few Red Cross volunteers, she crossed the war zone to reach the devastated hospital and evacuate young patients.
- Missionaries of Charity which was rejected by the Communist countries earlier, found an acceptance in the 1980s. Ever since it attained permission, the congregation initiated a dozen of projects. She helped the earthquake victims of Armenia, the famished folks of Ethiopia and the radiation-caused victims of Chernobyl.
- The first Missionaries of Charity home in the United States was established in the South Bronx, New York. By 1984, it had 19 establishments all over the country.
- In 1991, Mother Teresa returned to her homeland for the first time since 1937 and opened a Missionaries of Charity Brothers home in Tirana, Albania.
- By 1997, Missionaries of Charity had almost 4000 sisters working in 610 foundations, in 450 centres in 123 countries across the sIX continents. The congregation had several hospices and homes for people with HIV/AIDS, leprosy

Early Life of Mother T eresa **45**

and tuberculosis, soup kitchens, children's and family counselling programs, personal helpers, orphanages, and schools functioning under it.

A Vocation of Service

In 1952 the first Home for the Dying was opened in space made available by the City of Calcutta. Over the years, Mother Teresa's Missionaries of Charity grew from 12 to thousands serving the "poorest of the poor" in 450 centers around the world. Mother Teresa created many homes for the dying and the unwanted from Calcutta to New York to Albania. She was one of the pioneers of establishing homes for AIDS victims. For more than 45 years, Mother Teresa comforted the poor, the dying, and the unwanted around the world.

In 1966, the Missionaries of Charity Brothers was founded. Homes began to open in Rome, Tanzania, and Australia. In 1971, the first home in the United States was established in the South Bronx, New York.

Mother Teresa gained worldwide acclaim with her tireless efforts on behalf of world peace. Her work brought her numerous humanitarian awards, including : the Pope John XXIII Peace Prize and the Nobel Peace Prize in 1979. In receiving this award, Mother Teresa revolutionized the award ceremony. She insisted on a departure from the ceremonial banquet and asked that theFUNDS, $6,000 be donated to the poor in Calcutta. This money would permit her to feed hundreds for a year.

She is stated to have said that earthly rewards were important only if they helped her help the world's needy.

Beginning in 1980, homes began to spring-up for drug addicts, prostitutes, battered women, and more orphanages and schools for poor children around the world. In 1985, Mother Teresa established the first hospice for AIDS victims in New York. Later homes were added in San Francisco and Atlanta. Mother Teresa was awarded Medal of Freedom, the highest U.S. civilian award.

In 1991, Mother Teresa returned for the first time to her native Albania and opened a home in Tirana. By this year, there were 168 homes established in India.

46   *Mother Teresa*

On February 3, 1994 at a National Prayer Breakfast, sponsored by the U.S. Senate and House of Representatives, in Washington, DC, Mother Teresa challenged the audience on such topics as family life and abortion. She said, "Please don't kill the child. I want the child. Give the child to me."

Mother Teresa traveled to help the hungry in Ethiopia, radiation victims at Chernobyl, and earthquake victims in Armenia. Her zeal and works of mercy knew no boundaries.

In November of 1996, Mother Teresa received the honorary U.S. citizenship.

Her Words

A clean heart is a free heart. A free heart can love Christ with an undivided love in chastity, convinced that nothing and nobody will separate it from his love. Purity, chastity, and virginity created a special beauty in Mary that attracted God's attention. He showed his great love for the world by giving Jesus to her.

There is a terrible hunger for love. We all experience that in our lives - the pain, the loneliness. We must have the courage to recognize it. The poor you may have right in your own family.

Find them.

Love them.

Before you speak, it is necessary for you to listen, for God speaks in the silence of the heart.

Give yourself fully to God. He will use you to accomplish great things on the condition that you believe much more in His love than in your own weakness.

Speak tenderly to them. Let there be kindness in your face, in your eyes, in your smile, in the warmth of your greeting. Always have a cheerful smile. Don't only give your care, but give your heart as well.

The more you have, the more you are occupied, the less you give. But the less you have the more free you are. Poverty for us is a freedom. It is not mortification, a penance.

It is joyful freedom. There is no television here, no this, no that. But we are perfectly happy.

Early Life of Mother T eresa 47

I pray that you will understand the words of Jesus, "Love one another as I have loved you." Ask yourself "How has he loved me? Do I really love others in the same way?" Unless this love is among us, we can kill ourselves with work and it will only be work, not love. Work without love is slavery.

Little things are indeed little, but to be faithful in little things is a great thing.

A sacrifice to be real must cost, must hurt, must empty ourselves. The fruit of silence is prayer, the fruit of prayer is faith, the fruit of faith is love, the fruit of love is service, the fruit of service is peace.

QUOTES OF MOTHER TERESA

"Keep the joy of loving God in your heart and share this joy with all you meet especially your family. Be holy – let us pray."

"I once picked up a woman from a garbage dump and she was burning with fever; she was in her last days and her only lament was: 'My son did this to me.' I begged her: You must forgive your son. In a moment of madness, when he was not himself, he did a thing he regrets. Be a mother to him, forgive him. It took me a long time to make her say: 'I forgive my son.' Just before she died in my arms, she was able to say that with a real forgiveness. She was not concerned that she was dying. The breaking of the heart was that her son did not want her. This is something you and I can understand."

"When once a chairman of a multinational company came to see me, to offer me a property in Bombay, he first asked: 'Mother, how do you manage your budget?' I asked him who had sent him here. He replied: 'I felt an urge inside me.' I said: other people like you come to see me and say the same. It was clear God sent you, Mr. A, as He sends Mr. X, Mrs. Y, Miss Z, and they provide the material means we need for our work. The grace of God is what moved you. You are my budget. God sees to our needs, as Jesus promised. I accepted the property he gave and named it Asha Dan (Gift of Hope).

"Yesterday is gone. Tomorrow has not yet come. We have only today. Let us begin."

48 *Mother Teresa*

"Like Jesus we belong to the world living not for ourselves but for others. The joy of the Lord is our strength."

"There is only one God and He is God to all; therefore it is important that everyone is seen as equal before God.

I've always said we should help a Hindu become a better Hindu, a Muslim become a better Muslim, a Catholic become a better Catholic.

We believe our work should be our example to people. We have among us 475 souls - 30 families are Catholics and the rest are all Hindus, Muslims, Sikhs — all different religions. But they all come to our prayers."

"There are so many religions and each one has its different ways of following God. I follow Christ:

Jesus is my God,

Jesus is my Spouse,

Jesus is my Life,

Jesus is my only Love,

Jesus is my All in All;

Jesus is my Everything."

Make us worthy, Lord, to serve those people throughout the world who live and die in poverty and hunger. Give them through our hands, this day, their daily bread, and by our understanding love, give them peace and joy.

I heard the call to give up all and follow Christ into the slums to serve Him among the poorest of the poor. It was an order.

I was to leave the convent and help the poor while living among them.

When a poor person dies of hunger, it has not happened because God did not take care of him or her.

It has happened because neither you nor I wanted to give that person what he or she needed.

You and I, we are the Church, no? We have to share with our people. Suffering today is because people are hoarding, not giving, not sharing.

Early Life of Mother T eresa   **49**

Jesus made it very clear. Whatever you do to the least of my brethren, you do it to me.

Give a glass of water, you give it to me. Receive a little child, you receive me.

E verybody today seems to be in such a terrible rush, anxious for greater developments and greater riches and so on, so that children have very little time for their parents. Parents have very little time for each other, and in the home begins the disruption of peace of the world.

If we really want to love we must learn how to forgive.

Prayers and Meditations

Into Paradise

May the Angels lead her into Paradise.

May the Martyrs receive her at her coming and take her to Jerusalem, the Holy City.

May the Choirs of the Angels receive her, and may she, with the once poor Lazarus, have rest everlasting. Amen. -The Roman Ritual

For A Religious

All-powerful God, out of love for Christ and his Church, Mother Teresa served you faithfully in the religious life.

May she rejoice at the coming of your glory and enjoy eternal happiness with her sisters in your kingdom.

We ask this through our Lord Jesus Christ, your Son, who lives and reigns with you and the Holy Spirit, one God for ever and ever.

For A Woman Deceased

Lord, we beseech Thee, in the tenderness of Thy great mercy, to have pity upon the soul of Thy handmaid Mother Teresa, cleanse her from all defilements which have stained this mortal body, and give her inheritance in everlasting salvation. Through our Lord Jesus Christ, who with the Father and Holy Ghost liveth and reigneth world without end Amen.

50 *Mother Teresa*

Grant, O Lord, we beseech Thee, this mercy unto Thy servant deceased, that, having in desire kept Thy will, she may not suffer in requital of her deeds: and as a true Faith joined her unto the company of Thy faithful here below, so may Thy tender mercy give her place above, among the Angel choirs. Through Christ our Lord.

R. Amen.

V. Eternal rest grant unto her, O Lord.

R. And let perpetual light shine upon her.

V. May she rest in peace.

R. Amen.

V. May her soul, and the souls of all the faithful departed, through the mercy of God, rest in peace.

R. Amen.

To Thee, O Lord, do we commend the soul of Thy servant Mother Teresa, that being dead to the world she may live unto Thee; and whatsoever sins she has committed through the frailty of her mortal nature, do Thou, by the pardon of Thy most merciful love, wash away.

R. Amen.

O Almighty God, Judge of the living and the dead, so fit and prepare us, we beseech Thee, by Thy grace, for that last account which we must one day give; that, when the time of our appointed change shall come, we may look up to Thee with joy and comfort, and may at last be received, together with her whom Thou hast now taken from us, and with all that are near and dear to us, into that place of rest and peace where Thou shalt Thyself wipe away all tears from all eyes and where all our troubles and sorrows shall have an end, through the merits and for the sake of Jesus Christ, our Blessed Saviour and Redeemer. Amen

Prayer to the Heart of Jesus

Gentlest Heart of Jesus, ever present in the Blessed Sacrament, ever consumed with burning love for the poor captive souls in Purgatory, have mercy on the soul of Your departed servant.

Early Life of Mother T eresa   **51**

Be not severe in Your judgment, but let some drops of Your Precious Blood fall upon her, and send, O merciful Saviour, Your angels to conduct her to a place of refreshment, light and peace. Amen.

For the Poor

Make us worthy, Lord, to serve those people throughout the world who live and die in poverty and hunger. Give them through our hands, this day, their daily bread, and by our understanding love, give them peace and joy. -*Mother Teresa of Calcutta*

For the Helpless Unborn

Heavenly Father, You created mankind in Your own image and You desire that not even the least among us should perish. In Your love for us, You entrusted Your only Son to the holy Virgin Mary. Now, in Your love, protect against the wickedness of the evil, those little ones to whom You have given the gift of life.

PRAYER FOR A DECEASED PERSON

O God, Whose property it is ever to have mercy and to spare, we beseech Thee on behalf of the soul of Thy servant whom Thou hast called out of this world; look upon her with pity and let her be conducted by the holy angels to paradise, her true country. Grant that she who believed in Thee and hoped in Thee may not be left to suffer the pains of the purgatorial fire, but may be admitted to eternal joys. Through Jesus Christ, Thy Son, our Lord, Who with Thee and the Holy Ghost liveth and reigneth world without end. Amen.

Pray an Our Father followed by a Hail Mary.

V. Eternal rest give unto her, O Lord;

R. And let perpetual light shine upon her.

All powerful God, we pray for our sister Mother Teresa, who responded to the call of Christ and pursued wholeheartedly the ways of perfect love.

Grant that she may rejoice on that day when your glory will be revealed and in company with all her brothers and sisters share for ever the happiness of your kingdom.

52 *Mother Teresa*

We ask this through Christ our Lord.

Reflection of Teresa

"...I know that I join countless others across the world in giving thanks to God for the many contributions Mother Teresa has made to the Church and to the human family. Mother Teresa spent her life with the Lord, especially serving Him in the poor. She must be especially happy to meet Him now face to face. Her life's work is assured through her sisters, the Missionaries of Charity, to whom I offer my deepest sympathy – especially to the sistersw hos erveS t.M alachyPar isho nC hicago'sWes tS ide.T he simplicity of her lifestyle and the singlemindness of her dedication will serve as an example for generations to come. Believing in the power of God's grace which transformed her life, each of us – relying on the same grace—can do what she has done."

Archbishop Francis George, OMI, Archdiocese of Chicago

"We are here to grieve the loss of a precious jewel, a glorious crown and a golden heart in the Church."

Jaime Cardinal Sin, of the Philippines, at a Saturday evening Mass for Mother Teresa

"All the life of this great woman was the bright incarnation of service to the high humanitarian ideals of goodness, compassion, selflessness and faith. Mother Teresa will always remain in the hearts and minds of Russians as a friend of our country, ready to render help at any moment."

Russian President, Boris Yeltsin

Fr. Andrew Apostoli, CFR, Yonkers, NY re-counted his first meeting with Mother Teresa in New York. Fr. Andrew has given retreats for the Missionaries of Charity contemplative sisters in the South Bronx on several occasions. On our first meeting, Mother Teresa gave me a rosary and commented that "the Blessed Mother is all over the world bringing people to Her Son." She told me a story stating, "whenever I need a special favor, I do an Express Novena. An Express Novena is 9 Memorares in a row. In 1983, one of our Superior sisters had gotten sick in Eastern Berlin, and Mother Teresa had to appoint a replacement that could handle the

Early Life of Mother T eresa **53**

Communist government. The sister that they appointed as the successor for Eastern Berlin needed a Visa. Mother Teresa gathered her nuns and started praying the Express Novena (9 Memorare's). On the 8th Memorare, the phone rang, it was a Communist official stating that it would be 6 months until they would receive the Visa. After the 9th prayer, Mother Teresa started the novena again. On the 8th Memorare the second time, the telephone rang this time, it was a Communist official who stated you will have your Visa immediately!" Mother Teresa had a tremendous love for Our Lady. She had great courage and once stated to me that "I never refused God anything".

"When she walked into the room to greet me, I felt that I was indeed meeting a saint."

Evangelist, Billy Graham

"In an age when superlatives are used with abandon to describe the contributions of public figures, it is a testimony to Mother Teresa's greatness that no same person would give her the status as the world's most giving human being. But perhaps most of all, she will be remembered as someone who never sought the honor she so sincerely earned."

William Donohue, Catholic League President

"The passing of Mother Teresa is a moment of joy because of her holiness. She was always with the dying and the poor, so rather than bringing mourning it brings joy. We are happy to offer her to God: Here is such a lovely soul."

Bishop David E. Foley, Diocese of Birmingham, Alabama

The world marveled "at the commitment of this extraordinary woman."

Bishop Gerald R. Barnes of San Bernardino, CA.

"A loss to the entire humanity. She will be deeply missed in our efforts to build international peace, and a just, caring and equitable world order."

South African President Nelson Mandela's

"Mother Teresa imitated Christ and her life was a lesson in love. As she personally tended the sick and the dying in Calcutta's

54   *Mother Teresa*

slums, she helped people there and beyond see the material and spiritual poverty that confronts modern society. She taught all — from youth groups to governments — through piety and charm, wisdom and simplicity.

As small and soft-spoken as she was, her reach was large and her message heard around the world. She saw Jesus in everyone — from the child in the womb, to the sick and vulnerable, especially those afflicted with AIDS, to the aged and dying abandoned in the streets of Calcutta.

She urged people everywhere to reach beyond themselves to heal those hurting about them. Mother Teresa transcended cultures and politics as she spoke of God's call to love and assist the poor. She had a profound realization that anyone she was with — immigrant, alien, president or prime minister, was first of all a Child of God and intrinsically worthy of respect. Her life will stand as a reminder to all of us that we are called to care for one another and especially that we are called to respect and aid the poorest among us. God blesses the world with wonderful treasures — certainly Mother Teresa has been one of the finest of our century."

Bishop Anthony M. Pilla, President of the National Conference of Catholic Bishops/United States Catholic Conference

"Mother Teresa's life proved that the only real revolution in human affairs flows from service to others and self-sacrifice out of love for Jesus Christ. She was a champion of the unwanted, from the outcast of Calcutta to the unwanted unborn of America. She was the genius of the little way of doing great things. Above all, she was in every sense a woman of the Gospel: strong in forgiving, tender to the poor, in love with Jesus Christ, and a servant of His Church. May God welcome her into eternal light and joy, and may the work of her sisters here in Colorado and around the world thrive on the legacy of mercy and Christian love she leaves with us." Archbishop Charles J. Chaput, Archdiocese of Denver

"An example of selfless devotion to charity. I hope she can be a good example to all charity workers and philanthropists."

Early Life of Mother Teresa   **55**

Malaysian Prime Minister Mahathir Mohamad

"A rare and unique individual who lived long for higher purposes. Her life-long devotion to the care of the poor, the sick and the disadvantaged was one of the highest examples of service to humanity."

Nawaz Sharif, Prime Minister of Pakistan

The Chairman of the Nobel Peace Prize panel, Francis Sejersted, said Mother Teresa stood out "as an example of true self-sacrifice in humanitarian work." She was awarded the prize in 1979.

In a memorial Mass celebrating the life of Mother Teresa at St. Patrick Cathedral in New York on Monday, Cardinal John O'Connor spoke of the life of this devote nun who gave her life "fighting for the weakest of the weak, the poorest of the poor." On ministering to the poor Mother Teresa wrote, "Without suffering, our work would just be social work." O'Connor added, "Only by being one with them can we redeem them." Rudolph Giuliani, Mayor of NYC, shared with Mass attendees his thanks "for having had Mother Teresa among us." On a lighter note, Mayor Giuliani commented that he and former Mayor Ed Koch never said no when Mother Teresa asked the city [New York] for help. "We knew she knew better than us what's good for our people," Giuliani said. "If she wanted parking spaces, we gave her parking spaces."

Albania on Saturday declared three days of mourning next week to honor Mother Teresa, who was of Albanian descent. The red flag bearing the black double-headed eagle would fly at half-staff from Saturday through to the end of the national mourning period. Condolence books would be opened in all Albanian embassies.

Awards & Achievements

- For her unwavering commitment and unflinching love and compassion that she devoutly shared, the Government of India honoured her with Padma Shri, Jawaharlal Nehru Award for International Understanding and Bharat Ratna, India's highest civilian award.

56   *Mother Teresa*

- In 1962, she was honoured with Ramon Magsaysay Award for International Understanding, for her merciful cognizance of the abject poor of a foreign land, in whose service she led a new congregation.
- In 1971, she was awarded the first Pope John XXIII Peace Prize for her work with the poor, display of Christian charity and efforts for peace.
- In 1979, Mother Teresa was awarded the Nobel Peace Prize, "for work undertaken in the struggle to overcome poverty and distress, which also constitutes a threat to peace."

Death & Legacy

- Mother Teresa's health started declining in the 1980s. The first instance of the same was seen when she suffered a heart attack while visiting Pope John Paul II in Rome in 1983.
- For the next decade, Mother Teresa constantly faced health issues. Cardiac problems seemed to live by her, as she experienced no respite even after heart surgery.
- Her declining health led her to step down as the head of the order on March 13, 1997. Her last visit abroad was to Rome, when she visited Pope John Paul II for the second time.
- Upon returning to Calcutta, Mother Teresa spent her last few days receiving visitors and instructing sisters. The greatly compassionate soul left for the heavenly abode on September 5, 1997. Her death was mourned by the world over.
- The world has commemorated this saintly soul through various ways. She has been memorialized and has been made patroness of various churches. There are also several roads and structures that have been named after Mother Teresa. She has also been seen in popular cultures.
- In 2003, Mother Teresa was beautified by Pope John Paul II at St Peter's Basilica, in Vatican City. Since then, she has been known as Blessed Mother Teresa. Along with

Early Life of Mother T eresa   **57**

Blessed Pope John Paul II, the Church designated Blessed Teresa of Calcutta as the patron saint of the World Youth Day.

MISSIONARIES OF CHARITY

Missionaries of Charity is a Roman Catholic Latin Rite religious congregation established in 1950 by Mother Teresa. It consists of over 4,501religious sistersan d is active in 133 countries. Members of the order designate their affiliation using the order's initials, "M.C." A member of the Congregation must hear to the vows of chastity, poverty, obedience, and the fourth vow, to give "wholehearted free service to the poorest of the poor."

Today, the order consists of both Contemplative and Active Branches of Brothers and Sisters over several different countries. In 1963, both the Contemplative branch of the Sisters and the Active branch of the Brothers were founded, Brothers being co-founded by then Australian Jesuit(who became Brother Andrew, M.C.) Fr Ian Travers-Ball S.J. In 1979 the Contemplative branch of the Brothers was added and in 1984 a priest branch, the Missionaries of Charity Fathers, was founded by Mother Teresa with Fr. Joseph Langford, combining the vocation of the Missionaries of Charity with the Ministerial Priesthood. As with the Sisters, the Fathers live a very simple lifestyle without television, radios or items of convenience. They neither smoke nor drink alcohol and beg for their food. They make a visit to their families every five years but do not take annual holidays. Lay Catholics and non-Catholics constitute the Co-Workers of Mother Teresa, the Sick and Suffering Co-Workers, and the Lay Missionaries of Charity.

Missionaries care for those who include refugees, ex-prostitutes, the mentally ill, sick children, abandoned children, lepers, people with AIDS, theaged, and convalescent. They have schools run by volunteers to educate street children, they run soup kitchens, as many other services as per the communities' needs. They have 19 homes in Kolkata (Calcutta) alone which include homes for women, for orphaned children, and for the dying; an AIDS hospice, a school for street children,

58 *Mother Teresa*

and a leper colony. These services are provided, without charge, to people regardless of their religion or social caste.

In 1990, Mother Teresa asked to resign as head of the Missionaries, but was soon voted back in as Superior General. On March 13, 1997, six months before Mother Teresa's death, Sister Mary Nirmala Joshiw as selected the new Superior General of the Missionaries of Charity. SisterMary Prema was elected to succeed Sister Nirmala during a general chapter held in Calcutta in April 2009.

Foundation

On October 7, 1950, Mother Teresa and the small community formed by her former pupils was labeled as the *Diocesan Congregation of the Calcutta Diocese*, and thus received the permission from the Vaticanto exist as a Church subject. Their mission was to care for (in Mother Teresa's words) "the hungry, the naked, the homeless, the crippled, the blind, the lepers, all those people who feel unwanted, unloved, uncared for throughout society, people that have become a burden to the society and are shunned by everyone." It began as a small community with 12 members in Calcutta, and today it has over 4,500 Sisters running orphanages, AIDS hospices, charity centres worldwide, and caring for refugees, the blind, disabled, aged, alcoholics, the poor and homeless and victims of floods, epidemics and famine in Asia, Africa, Latin America,North America, Europe and Australia.

In 1965, by granting a Decree of Praise, Pope Paul VI granted Mother Teresa's request to expand her congregation to other countries. The Congregation started to grow rapidly, with new homes opening all over the globe. The congregation's first house outside India was in Venezuela, and others followed in Rome and Tanzania, and eventually in many countries in Asia, Africa, and Europe, including Albania. In addition, the first home of the Missionaries of Charity in the United States was established in the South Bronx, New York. In the USA, the Missionaries of Charity are affiiated with the Council of Major Superiors of Women Religious, a body of female religious, representing 20% of American nuns. They are identified by the wearing of religious habits, and

Early Life of Mother T eresa   **59**

loyalty to church teaching. By 1996, the Organisation was operating 517 missions in more than 100 countries and today is assisted by over one million co-workers and many donations from ordinary people.

Becoming a Missionary of Charity

It takes nine years to become a full-fledged Missionary of Charity. At the beginning, anyone interested in the life can come for a short term "come-and-see" experience. If the young women still wish to join and are still considered possible candidates by the Congregation, they enter Aspirancy, focused on learning English (which is the community language) for those who are not from English-speaking countries and deepening of their Christian life.

It is followed by Postulancy (introduction into the study of the SacredScripture, the Constitutions of the Society, Church history, and Theology. If found suitable, they enter the Novitiate, which is the true beginning of the religious life. Novices wear white cotton habit with a girdle and white saris without the three blue stripes. In the first year (called canonical), they deepen their life of prayer and relationship with God along with their knowledge of life as a Missionary of Charity, the second year is more focused on the practical training for the mission life. After two years, they take temporary vows for one year, which are renewed annually (five years in total). They also receive the blue striped sario f the Congregation and a metal crucifix as a sign of their spousal love for Christ. In the sixth year, they travel to Rome, Calcutta or Washington D.C. for "Tertianship", a year of deep spiritual growth, at the end of which they make their final profession.

Material goods

A Sister's few possessions include: three saris (one to wear, one to wash, one to mend); two or three cotton habits; a girdle; a pair of sandals; a crucifix; and a rosary. They also have a plate, a set of cutlery, a cloth napkin, a canvas bag, and a prayer book. In cold countries, nuns may own a cardigan and other articles suited to the local climate such as a coat, scarf, and closed shoes.

Quality of care provided in the Home for the Dying in Kolkata

The quality of care offered to terminally ill patients in the Home for the Dying in Kolkata was the subject of discussion in the mid-1990s. Some British observers, on the basis of short visits, drew unfavourable comparisons with the standard of care available in hospices in the United Kingdom. Remarks made by Dr. Robin Fox relative to the lack of full-time medically-trained personnel and the absence of strong analgesics were published in a brief memoir in an issue of *The Lancet* in 1994. These remarks were criticised in a later issue of *The Lancet* on the ground that they failed to take account of Indian conditions, specifically the fact that government regulations effectively precluded the use of morphine outside large hospitals. A British former volunteer at the Home objected that syringes were rinsed in cold water and reused; that inmates were given cold baths; and that aspirin was administered to people with terminal cancer. Fox made no reference to any of these practices, but noted that the inmates were "eating heartily and doing well", and that the sisters and volunteers focused on cleanliness, tending wounds and sores, and providing loving kindness. The use of aspirin to relieve mild to moderate pain in those suffering terminal cancer remains standard practice worldwide as approved by the WHO. The life-span of a sterilizable needle and syringe was estimated in 1995 to be between 50 and 200 injections depending on the hardness of local water.

3

Criticism of Mother Teresa

This article concerns the Albanian-born Roman Catholic nun and missionary Mother Teresa and examines some of the criticism lodged against her. For a more complete picture of the person, see the article Mother Teresa.

CRITICISM FROM THE MEDIA

An Indian-born writer living in Britain, Aroup Chatterjee, who had briefly worked in one of Mother Teresa's homes, began investigations into the finances and other practices of Teresa's order. In 1994, two British journalists, Christopher Hitchens and Tariq Ali, produced a critical British Channel 4 documentary, *Hell's Angel*, based on Chatterjee's work.

The next year, Hitchens published *The Missionary Position: Mother Teresa in Theory and Practice*, a pamphlet which repeated many of the accusations in the documentary. Chatterjee himself published *The Final Verdict* in 2003, a less polemic work than those of Hitchens and Ali, but equally critical of Teresa's operations.

Support of Indira Gandhi

After Indian Prime Minister Indira Gandhi's suspension of civil liberties in 1975, Mother Teresa said: "People are happier. There are more jobs. There are no strikes." These approving comments were seen as a result of the friendship between Teresa and the Congress Party. Mother Teresa's comments were even criticized outside India within Catholic media. (Chatterjee, p. 276.)

Stance on abortion

From the early 1970s, Mother Teresa began to attract some criticism. Many advocates of the family planning and pro-choice movements were critical of her views and influence because she was opposed to artificial contraception and abortion. Mother

62   *Mother Teresa*

Teresa frequently spoke against them publicly and in meetings with high level government officials. In her Nobel Prize acceptance speech, she declared, "Abortion is the worst evil, and the greatest enemy of peace... Because if a mother can kill her own child, what will prevent us from killing ourselves or one another? Nothing."

In the aftermath of the Indo-Pakistani War of 1971, it was determined that more than 450,000 Hindu women in East Pakistan (now Bangladesh) had been systematically raped. Even in these circumstances she asserted her rejection of abortion by publicly denouncing abortion as an option and by calling upon the women left behind to keep their unborn children. She characterized her views later when asked in 1993 about a 14-year-old rape victim in Ireland, "Abortion can never be necessary... because it is pure killing."

This stance is in line with that of the Roman Catholic Church, which asserts natural family planning is the only acceptable form of birth control, even in cases where conception is the result of sexual abuse or rape.

Baptisms of the dying

Mother Teresa encouraged members of her order to baptize dying patients, without regard to the individual's religion. In a speech at the Scripps Clinic in California in January 1992, she said: "Something very beautiful... not one has died without receiving the special ticket for St. Peter, as we call it. We call baptism ticket for St. Peter. We ask the person, do you want a blessing by which your sins will be forgiven and you receive God? They have never refused. So 29,000 have died in that one house [in Kalighat] from the time we began in 1952."

Critics have argued that patients were not provided sufficient information to make an informed decision about whether they wanted to be baptized and the theological significance of a Christian baptism.

Some of Mother Teresa's defenders have argued that baptisms are either soul-saving or harmless and hence the criticisms would be pointless (a variant ofPas cal's Wager). Simon Leys, in a letter to the *New York Review of Books*, wrote: "Either you believe in the

Criticism of Mother Teresa

supernatural effect of this gesture – and then you should dearly wish for it. Or you do not believe in it, and the gesture is as innocent and well-meaningly innocuous as chasing a fly away with a wave of the hand."

Questionable relationships

In 1981, Teresa flew to Haiti to accept the Legion d'Honneur from the right-wing dictator Jean-Claude Duvalier, who, after his ouster, was found to have stolen millions of dollars from the impoverished country. There she said that the Duvaliers "loved their poor", and that "their love was reciprocated".

Criticism was leveled at what some perceived to be Mother Teresa's endorsement of the aggressively atheist regime of Enver Hoxha in communist Albania. She had visited Albania in August 1989, where she was received by Hoxha's widow, Nexhmije, Foreign Minister Reis Malile, Minister of Health, Ahmet Kamberi, the Chairman of the People's Assembly Petro Dode, and other state and party officials.

She subsequently laid a bouquet on Hoxha's grave, and placed a wreath on the statue of Mother Albania, without commenting on the Albanian Communist party's human rights violations and suppression of religion. However, her supporters defended such associations, saying she had to deal with political realities of the time in order to lobby for her causes. By the time of her death, the Missionaries of Charity had houses in most Communist countries.

She accepted money from the British publisher Robert Maxwell, who, as was later revealed, embezzled UK£450 million from his employees' pension funds. There is no suggestion that she was aware of any theft before accepting the donation in either case. Criticism does focus on Teresa's plea for leniency in the Charles Keating case. Keating donated millions of dollars to Mother Teresa and lent her his private jet when she visited the United States. She refused to return the money, and praised Keating repeatedly. There has been a lack of media investigation of her relationships to these individuals, though Christopher Hitchens was a strident critic.

64 *Mother Teresa*

She supported Licio Gelli's nomination for the Nobel Prize in Literature. Gelli is known for being the head of the Propaganda Due masonic lodge, which was implicated in various murders and high-profile corruption cases in Italy, as well as having close connections with the neo-fascist Italian Social Movement and the Argentine Military Junta.

MOTIVATION OF CHARITABLE ACTIVITIES

Chatterjee stated that the public image of Mother Teresa as a "helper of the poor" was misleading, and that only a few hundred people are served by even the largest of the homes. In 1998, among the 200 charitable assistance organizations reported to operate in Calcutta, Missionaries of Charity was not ranked among the largest charity organizations–with the Assembly of God charity notably serving a greater number of the poor at 18,000 meals daily.

Chatterjee alleged that many operations of the order engage in no charitable activity at all but instead use their funds for missionary work. He stated, for example, that none of the eight facilities that the Missionaries of Charity run in Papua New Guinea have any residents in them, being purely for the purpose of converting local people to Catholicism.

She was sometimes accused by Hindus in her adopted country of trying to convert the poor to Catholicism by "stealth". Christopher Hitchens described Mother Teresa's organization as a cult which promoted suffering and did not help those in need. He said that Mother Teresa's own words on poverty proved that her intention was not to help people, quotingh erw ordsat a1981 press conference in which she was asked: "Do you teach the poor to endure their lot?" She replied: "I think it is very beautiful for the poor to accept their lot, to share it with the passion of Christ. I think the world is being much helped by the suffering of the poor people."

Quality of medical care

In 1991, Robin Fox, editor of the British medical journal *The Lancet* visited the Home for Dying Destitutes in Calcutta (now Kolkata) and described the medical care the patients received

Criticism of Mother T eresa

as "haphazard". He observed that sisters and volunteers, some of whom had no medical knowledge, had to make decisions about patient care, because of the lack of doctors in the hospice. Fox specifically held Teresa responsible for conditions in this home, and observed that her order did not distinguish between curable and incurablepatients, so that people who could otherwise survive would be at risk of dying from infections and lack of treatment.

Fox conceded that the regimen he observed included cleanliness, the tending of wounds and sores, and kindness, but he noted that the sisters' approach to managing pain was "disturbingly lacking". The formulary at the facility Fox visited lacked strong analgesics which he felt clearly separated Mother Teresa's approach from the hospice movement. Fox also wrote that needles were rinsed with warm water, which left them inadequately sterilized, and the facility did not isolate patients with tuberculosis. There have been a series of other reports documenting inattention to medical care in the order's facilities. Similar points of view have also been expressed by some former volunteers who worked for Teresa's order. Mother Teresa herself referred to the facilities as "Houses of the Dying".

Destination of donations

It has been alleged by former employees of Mother Teresa's order that Teresa refused to authorize the purchase of medical equipment, and that donated money was instead transferred to the Vatican Bank for general use, even if it was specifically earmarked for charitable purposes. See Missionaries of Charity for a detailed discussion of these allegations. Mother Teresa did not disclose her order's financial situation except where she was required to do so by law.

AS AN IMAGE OF COLONIALISM AND RACISM

In *White Women in Racialized Spaces: Imaginative Transformation and Ethical Action in Literature*, Samina Najmi and Rajini Srikanth said of Mother Teresa:

Mother Teresa is the quintessential image of the white woman in the colonies, working to save the dark bodies from their own

66   *Mother Teresa*

temptations and failures. [...] The Euro-American dominated international media continue to harbor the colonial notion that white people are somehow especially endowed with the capacity to create social change. When nonwhite people labor in this direction, the media typically search for white benefactors or teachers, or else, for white people who stand in the wings to direct the nonwhite actors. Dark bodies cannot act of their own volition to stretch their own capacity, for they must wait, the media seem to imply, for some colonial administrator, or some technocrat from the IBM or the IMF to tell them how to do things. When it comes to saving the poor, the dark bodies are again invisible, for the media seem to celebrate when the worn out platitudes of such as Mother Teresa and ignore the struggles of those bodies for their own liberation. To open the life of someone like Mother Teresa to scrutiny, therefore, is always difficult. [...] Mother Teresa's work was part of a global enterprise for the alleviation of bourgeois guilt, rather than a genuine challenge to those forces that produce and maintain poverty.

Posthumous criticisms

Mother Teresa died in 1997. Despite her request that all writing and correspondence be destroyed, a collection was posthumously released to the public in book form. Her writings revealed that she struggled with feelings of disconnectedness that were in contrast to the strong feelings she had experienced as a young novice. In her letters Mother Teresa describes a decades long sense of feeling disconnected from God and lacking the earlier zeal which had characterized her efforts to start the Missionaries of Charity. As a result of this, she was judged by some to have "ceased to believe". Because of these statements she has been posthumously criticized for hypocrisy.

The Showtime program *Penn & Teller: Bullshit!* has an episode titled "Holier than Thou" that criticizes Mother Teresa, as well as Mahatma Gandhi and the 14th Dalai Lama. The show criticizes Mother Teresa's controversial relationships with Charles Keating and the Duvalier family, as well as the quality of medical care in her home for the dying. Christopher Hitchens appears on, and narrates some of the episode.

Criticism of Mother Teresa 67

COMMEMORATIONS OF MOTHER TERESA

Mother Teresa of Kolkata formerly called as Calcutta - has been memorialized throughout the world in recognition of her work with the poor. During her lifetime this commemoration often took the form of awards and honorary degrees bestowed upon her. She has also been memorialized through museums and dedications of churches, roads and other structures.

Mother Teresa in Albania

- Mother Teresa Day *(Dita e Nënë Terezës)* on October 19 is a public holiday in Albania.
- The airport of Tirana, the capital of Albania, is the Tirana International Airport Nënë Tereza, named after Mother Teresa in 2002.
- The second largest square in Tirana, the largest being Skanderbeg Square, is named after Mother Teresa. A monument of Mother Teresa is also found there.
- The biggest civil hospital in Tirana is named after her.

THE SAINT WITHOUT A NATION

This chapter traces the extent to which Mother Teresa's first eighteen years in Skopje have been studied or ignored by her biographers, especially those writing for a Western audience. The texts studied include works written from the early 1970s to the present. Considerable attention is paid to the literature about the 1910–1928 period originating from the Balkans. The textual analysis provided is intended to explore some of the motives for the attention, or lack of it, several Mother Teresa experts pay to her early life, family, ethnicity and nationality. The works analysed are seen in the contexts of the time when they were written, the nature of the authors' interest in Mother Teresa and their affiliations to certain religions, countries, nationalities and ethnic groups.

Some of the issues that come to mind with regard to most internationally known figures are their nationality and ethnic origin. This is certainly the case with most past and present Nobel Peace Prize recipients. It is difficult to separate well-known leaders and human rights activists from their own countries or peoples. So, for

68   *Mother Teresa*

instance, Mohamed Anwar Al-Sadat is inseparable from Egypt, Lech Walesa from Poland, Menachem Begin, Yitzhak Rabin and Shimon Peres from Israel, Aung San Suu Kyi from Burma, Fredrik Willem De Klerk and Nelson Mandela from South Africa, Yasser Arafat from Palestine, and John Hume and David Trimble from Northern Ireland. Nationality and ethnicity appear to be strong identifying signifiers also for the Nobel Peace laureates of the cloth.

The Reverend Dr Martin Luther King Jr, is always associated with the United States of America, just as Archbishop Desmond Mpilo Tutu is with South Africa, and the 14th Dalai Lama (Tenzin Gyatso) with Tibet. The 1979 winner of the Nobel Peace Prize, however, seems to be an interesting exception to the axiomatic conclusion about the association between someone's place of birth and their celebrity status. Mother Teresa is probably one of the few twentieth-century dignitaries – religious or otherwise – whose country of origin and ethnicity are little known to many people. Throughout her lifetime and after her death her identity was and remains strongly associated with India. Considering the long time she spent in India, it is no surprise that several authors have attempted to study her figure and legacy in the context of her adopted country. Many of them make this clear in the titles of their studies where the word 'India' figures conspiciously.

Most people who have written books and produced biographies (pic-torial, authorized and unauthorized) and films (documentary, feature and animated) on Mother Teresa, however, tend to accompany her name in the titles of their works especially with that of the city which became her home for some seventy years as a missionary. This tradition has its genesis in 1971 when Malcolm Muggeridge published his seminal work *Something Beautiful for God: Mother Teresa of Calcutta*. Since that time 'Calcutta' has become a fixture in the titles of numerous works on Mother Teresa.Some writers like Edward Le Joly (1985) and Sunita Kumar (1998) prefer to call their works on the nun simply *Mother Teresa of Calcutta*, with no other trimmings in the title.

Over the years, most of the nun's numerous ghost-writers have acknow-ledged her 'authorship' simply as 'Mother Teresa'.

Criticism of Mother Teresa

Some of them, however, feel that it is necessary to clarify that the 'author' of their works is not just any 'Mother Teresa' but *the* 'Mother Teresa of Calcutta'. This tendency, which began in the 1970s, became more apparent in the 1980s and the 1990s and has continued after her death.

Mother Teresa has been identified with Calcutta not only by the authors who admire her. Several of her critics also mention Calcutta in the titles of their works to highlight the alleged negative impact she started having on this city from the late 1960s when she first attracted the attention of the Western media. In April 1992, for instance, *The Nation* ran Christopher Hitchens's article 'The Ghoul of Calcutta'.

As for Mother Teresa's native country and her ethnic roots, however, they are never mentioned in the title of any work about her. It appears as if Mother Teresa of Calcutta had no country of origin or ethnicity in the conventional sense or, perhaps, no original homeland or ethnic connections worth mentioning. Apart from being 'Mother Teresa of Calcutta', the only other 'identity' ascribed to Mother Teresa is that of a Roman Catholic.

Mother Teresa's 'lack' of a conventional nationality is an indication of her popularity and enduring appeal, something which her supporters are always eager to emphasize. How such a highly publicized religious woman ended up with no definite national identity, though, is an issue they are not very keen to explore. The nun's numerous sympathetic image-makers of different religious, political and ethnic denominations apparently find in her an idealist who, like Stephen Dedalus, James Joyce's hero of the 1916 autobiographical novel *A Portrait of the Artist as a Young Man*, aimed at and apparently managed to rise above and 'fly by' the restricting 'nets' of nationality, language and politics. Unlike Joyce's artistic *doppelgänger*, however, Mother Teresa could reach out to people and celebrate life from within the 'net' of religion. With her lifetime commitment to help the poorest of the poor in a predominantly Hindu country like India, she succeeded in proving to a materialistic and largely sceptical West that religion can be used to improve people's spiritual and material well-being. The nun also showed that rather than dividing people, faith can bring

70   *Mother Teresa*

together communities across the cultural, ethnic, religious, economic and political divide.

Missing facts

Mother Teresa may indeed, to use a cliché, belong to India, but she was not an Indian. It is also important to emphasize that she had a separate identity from her fellow European Catholic missionaries in India. As stated earlier, Mother Teresa was an Albanian Catholic nun born and raised in Skopje, the capital of the recently independent state of Macedonia. This particular biographical detail has been acknowledged in Mother Teresa scholarship even before the bitter Balkan row over her ethnicity on the eve of the beatification. Mother Teresa's Albanian origin is mentioned in many books on the nun, whether they are penned by Indians or Westerners, friends or opponents, Christians or non-Christians, believers or nonbelievers. What Mother Teresa experts fail to acknowledge, however, is the significant role ethnic roots and national identity played in her life. These remain topics of merely casual interest in Mother Teresa scholarship to this day.

Agnes Gonxhe Bojaxhiu lived in Skopje up until 26 September 1928 when she left for Dublin to train as a nun. She would not return to her native city for almost half a century. An informed and impartial Mother Teresa scholar, however, would easily notice in the kind of Christianity she preached and in the charity work she carried out in India and throughout the world that, in a sense, she seemed never to have left Skopje. As we shall see later in this chapter and in the coming chapters, she carried with her much of the teachings that her parents, relatives and priests gave her in Skopje during her childhood and youth. Most of Mother Teresa's biographers pay no attention to her early years. This is particularly the case with Western and Indian experts. Many of them have not cared to visit her birthplace, and very few have made any attempts to interview the people who knew her during the 1910–1928 period.

Mother Teresa scholars who pay some attention to her early life and ethnic origin come mainly from the Balkans. Many of them are Albanians and Macedonian Slavs. As a rule, the Balkan writers are interested in the nun's childhood and youth mainly

Criticism of Mother T eresa **71**

because they apparently want to claim the famous nun as their own. This explains why Mother Teresa experts mushroomed in this region immediately after she was awarded the Nobel Peace Prize in 1979 and before the beatification in 2003.

Balkan biographers of the nun have failed to have any impact on the Mother Teresa literature produced in the West and India. Nor has the recent Balkan row over her ethnicity induced the large number of her non-Balkan sympathetic hagiographers and biographers, or her opponents, to pay attention to the years she spent in Skopje. Most of them are simply not interested in the formative stage of Mother Teresa's life or in the significance of her Albanian roots.

Mother Teresa is probably one of the most publicized twentieth-century figures and, with the exception of Pope John Paul II, certainly the most famous religious celebrity of our time. She was thrown into the limelight initially in 1950 when she was spotted by the Indian Catholic press in Calcutta. Both Catholic and non-Catholic Indian outlets ensured that she was constantly in the public eye, first in West Bengal and gradually throughout India. Thanks to the constant attention of the Indian media industry, and the equally constant backing of the Indian political estab-lishment, Mother Teresa's popularity in the subcontinent grew increasingly throughout the 1950s and especially after she became a world celebrity.

Several Indian journalists who covered Mother Teresa before she became famous in the West and thereafter would occasionally refer to her ethnicity. Some of them reported that the nun was originally Albanian. In most cases, however, they would simply remark that Mother Teresa was a Yugoslav nun. When she was alive, as a rule, Indian reporters and biog-raphers were not interested in her life before she set foot in their country. For most Indian writers Mother Teresa apparently had only one identity – that of a European Roman Catholic. As for her country of origin, ethnicity and, indeed, the first eighteen years of her life in Skopje, they were ignored almost completely. This trend has hardly changed in the literature on Mother Teresa that has come out in India in the wake of her death in 1997.

72   *Mother Teresa*

Mother Teresa's name and fame reached Western Europe not via India and the Vatican but through the United States. She was initially noticed by the American Catholic media apparatus towards the end of the 1950s. Catholic Americans took her to their hearts because of her services to the Catholic Church in a predominantly non-Catholic country like India. Several White House administrations like that of President Reagan, Ameri-can multinationals, like the now-defunct Union Carbide, and American businessmen like the financier Charles Keating, found in Mother Teresa a staunch ally in their hour of need.

Mother Teresa's first visit to Europe since 1928 took place in 1960. By that time, however, she was still relatively unknown in Europe. Euro-pean media started to pay attention to Mother Teresa mainly in the late 1960s.

Like her Indian admirers, Western journalists and writers have never shown any interest in highlighting Mother Teresa's ethnic roots and country of origin. This is obvious especially in the media coverage she received in Britain from 1968 when she was interviewed by Malcolm Muggeridge of the BBC. In 1969 Muggeridge made a film about Mother Teresa, choosing for a title one of her 'catchphrases' *Something Beautiful for God*. Two years later Muggeridge published a book on Mother Teresa – *Something Beautiful for God: Mother Teresa of Calcutta* – which proved to be one of the most influential image-making works on her. Since then she has been the subject of numerous books and television programmes. Even by the time she became world famous, her Albanian origin and early years were hardly of interest to the nun's biographers, whose number would increase considerably after she was awarded the Nobel Prize.

Mother Teresa's life may indeed have been 'public property' when she was alive. Strangely enough, however, unlike other international celeb-rities, in spite of the intense global media attention she received from the late 1970s until the end of the 1990s, nothing of importance was ever reported about her childhood.

This particular period was largely ignored and continues to be ignored in the ever-growing Mother Teresa literature intended

Criticism of Mother Teresa 73

primarily for Western readers. While the Western public is spared no minute details about almost every aspect of the charitable work carried out by Mother Teresa and her sisters and brothers of the Missionaries of Charity, the information about her as a child, as well as details about her schooling, social life and, equally important, about her parents and siblings remain sketchy, fragmented and, in most cases, missing altogether, even in some of the best biographies.

One of the reasons why, perhaps, some biographers skip Mother Teresa's early life completely or depict a very sketchy picture of her child-hood and youth is because they are apparently not fully aware of the importance of studying every stage of her life in offering as complete a portrait as possible of the person she really was. A considerable number of her early biographers had not written a proper biographical work or a book prior to taking upon themselves the task of chronicling her life. This is how Kathryn Spink records her gratitude to Mother Teresa about twenty years after the nun had given her the consent to write about her:

[Mother Teresa] gave me her permission to write, telling me that I did not have to ask, and adding that she hoped that I was not putting any of my own money into the venture. Apparently, Nobel laureate though she was, she had no inkling that her consent to that, my 'real'4first book with all its defects and limitations, would be enough to launch my career as a writer.

Mother Teresa launched, and probably will continue to launch, the careers of many other inexperienced biographers.

Of course, not every biography of Mother Teresa should cover her entire life. It is perfectly normal for some biographers to concentrate on certain stages of her life and work and either ignore or mention the others only in passing. This is often the case with biographies of famous people. What separates the biographies of MotherT eresaf romt heb iographicalw orkso no therw ell-known personalities is that, so far, almost none of her numerous biographers has made the nun's early years the sole or the main topic of their work. Even books with promising titles such as David Porter's *Mother Teresa: The Early Years* (1986) and Claire Jordan Mohan's *The Young Life of Mother Teresa of Calcutta* (1996)

74   *Mother Teresa*

would disappoint anyone expecting to find there a systematic and detailed account of Mother Teresa's childhood and youth. Rather than chronicling the early life of Agnes Gonxhe Bojaxhiu, Porter and Mohan are more interested in covering her life story after she left Skopje in 1928.

The tendency to pay little attention to Mother Teresa's early years is apparent not only in these works. Even the most prolific and seasoned Mother Teresa experts, Kathryn Spink included, fail to cover at length the nun's early life. In this context, in Mother Teresa scholarship, the word 'biography' is often a misnomer. Most of her biographies are simply hagiographies. As for Mother Teresa's opponents, they make casual remarks not so much about her early life as to the fact that she was Albanian.

Even in this case, her 'Albanianness' becomes an issue only when, like Christopher Hitchens, they want to highlight how 'devoted' she was to Albania and the Albanian national cause, or, like several Indian critics, they argue that, coming from a poor country like Albania, she should have tried to help her own impoverished compatriots first before taking it upon herself to alleviate the sufferings of vulnerable Indians.

On the whole, the literature on Mother Teresa bears the signature of her Catholic colleagues, friends, admirers and followers, which explains to some extent the predominantly devotional nature of their work. In spite of the fact that so many books have been churned out on this particular nun, it is still too early to talk about a dispassionate and objec-tive Mother Teresa scholarship. A few publications that appeared throughout the 1990s, and especially some that have come out in the wake of her death, however, are clear indications of a welcome tendency to study her life and work in a more detached way.

Even in this emerging non-partisan literature on Mother Teresa's person and legacy, there is no difference in the attitude towards her early life. Mother Teresa appears to be one of the public figures of our time about whom we seem to know almost everything as an adult but hardly anything of importance about her first eighteen years. So much so that it seems as if this religious celebrity was born at eighteen.

Criticism of Mother Teresa   **75**

A CATALOGUE OF BIOGRAPHICAL INACCURACIES

The little information Indian and Western writers provide about Mother Teresa's years in Skopje from 1910 to 1928 is full of inaccuracies. On the whole, Mother Teresa experts, who show no particular interest in her early years, also display some confusion about Agnes Gonxhe Bojaxhiu's actual birthplace as well as about the geography and history of the Balkans. In his article '"Mother" Teresa', Ken Matto locates her place of birth 'in what is now Yugoslavia/Bosnia'. According to David Porter, the nun was born 'in Skopje in Serbia'. On the opening page of his book *Life Stories: Mother Teresa*, Wayne Jackman observes that the town where Mother Teresa was born was 'Skopje in Macedonia'. In her study *Mother Teresa:*

The Nun Whose 'Mission of Love' Has Helped Millions of the World's Poorest People, Charlotte Gray notes that Mother Teresa was born 'in Skopje, Albania'.

The fact of the matter is that Mother Teresa was not born in Bosnia, Serbia, Macedonia or Albania, as we understand these terms now, or indeed as they were understood in the 1910s. Some opponents and admirers apparently fail to notice that for some five centuries before, and at least two more years after Agnes Gonxhe Bojaxhiu was born, Skopje was administered by the Ottoman Empire. The 'states' of Bosnia, Macedonia and Albania did not exist in 1910.

As for Serbia, this Balkan country had not yet occupied Mother Teresa's native city by the time she was born, nor did the European powers recognize the authority of the Serbian state over Macedonia during the eighteen years Mother Teresa lived in Skopje. To this day, Serbia has no legitimate territorial claim over Skopje or the new state of Macedonia. Historical and geographical inaccuracies of the same nature also surface in Richard Tames's book *Mother Teresa*.

According to Tames, the Skopje of 1910 was 'in the small kingdom of Serbia'. The kingdom of Serbia had no control over Skopje or 'Macedonia' throughout the long presence of the

76   *Mother Teresa*

Ottomans in the Balkans. Under the Turks, Skopje was included in the *vilÇyet* (the Turkish for 'administrative province') of Kosova, which was one of the four *vilÇyets* populated by the Albanians. The other three administrative provinces in the Albanian lands were those of Shkodër, Janinë and Manastir.

This is not the only inaccuracy recorded in Tames's book. In the opening pages of this work we are offered some information on the whereabouts of the shrine of the Madonna of Letnice. By all accounts, this religious place was very important to Mother Teresa throughout the first eighteen years of her life. Tames locates this well-known church not in Letnice, Kosova, but in another part of the Balkans altogether: 'The Bojaxhiu family prayed together every day, celebrated all the religious festivals and made a pilgrimage each year to the shrine of the Madonna of Letnice in the mountains of Montenegro.' The picture used to illustrate the location of this place of pilgrimage has this caption: 'Montenegro, a beautiful setting for the shrine of the Madonna of Letnice'. In her 2003 book on Mother Teresa, Emma Johnson also wrongly notes that the Madonna of Letnice shrine is in the mountains of Montenegro. Tames and Johnson obviously thought that since this place of worship is situated in a place called *crne gore*, which in Serbo-Croat means 'black mountain', and since there is a small state in the Balkans of the same name, then it stands to reason that the Bojaxhius went on their annual pilgrimage to Montenegro.

A few biographers make no reference at all to Mother Teresa's ethnic origin. Wayne Jackman (1993), for instance, mentions nothing about her being Albanian, not only in the opening chapter where he records some details about her parents and siblings, but also throughout the whole book.

It is not uncommon for Mother Teresa to be given a 'collective' and in-accurate ethnicity and nationality. In several publications she is referred to as a Yugoslav nun, who was born 'in Skopje, Yugoslavia'. Mother Teresa biographers like Malcolm Muggeridge, Georges Gorrée, Jean Barbier, Desmond Doig, Kathryn Spink, Eileen Egan and Kathleen Egan apparently fail to notice that there was no such place as 'Yugoslavia' at the time Mother Teresa was born. In its embryonic form, Yugoslavia emerged only in December

Criticism of Mother T eresa 77

1918, and even then its official name was the 'Kingdom of the Serbs, Croats and Slovenes'.

The fact that Mother Teresa was occasionally identified by the Indian and Western media as a 'Yugoslav' nun has led some people to believe that she was a Slav. This is how the Indian biographer Navin Chawla presents the relationship between the nun and Pope John Paul II in his 1992 book:

Quite understandably, her relations with the Head of the Catholic Church, Pope John Paul II, are very good. She invariably refers to him as 'Holy Father' and looks upon him as a real father. She admires his simplicity. She deeply appreciated his offering a place to the Missionaries of Charity in the Vatican, where they have set up a soup kitchen for the destitute of Rome. Not only does it serve as an acknow-ledgment of the presence of the poor, it has helped to demystify the aura of the Vatican as an oasis of great splendour and wealth. *Whether the fact that both are Slavs – he is Polish and she is a Yugoslav Albanian – has contributed to their mutual understanding and respect is a matter for conjecture.* The Pope certainly holds her in great regard, and admires her for her outspoken defence of the Church's traditional values. (emphasis added)

Chawla is right about Karol Wojtyla (the original name of Pope John Paul II) being a Slav. The 264th pontiff was a Pole who loved Poland dearly and who did everything he could to help his nation overthrow Communism. Like several other Mother Teresa biographers, however, Chawla obviously does not know much about the ethnic map of the Balkans.

Agnes Bojaxhiu was not a Slav, nor are her fellow Albanians. This explains why, in contrast to other nationalities living in the Yugoslav state that emerged in the second decade of the twentieth century, the Albanians living there became officially Yugoslav citizens not from the start but in 1928. Even when they were recognized by law as 'Yugoslavs', they were soon to learn that their new citizenship was hardly a passport to equal rights. It was mainly because of their non-Slavic origin that the rulers of Belgrade treated the Albanians as second-class citizens from the inception of the federal state of Yugoslavia in the late 1910s to its collapse in the early 1990s.

78 *Mother Teresa*

Chawla is also wrong about Mother Teresa's Venetian connection. Both Mother Teresa's parents were ethnic Albanians. Contrary to Chawla's claim, the nun's mother did not come 'from *nearby* Venice' (emphasis added). Chawla's conclusion about the vicinity of these two European metropolises is wrong not only in geographical terms, though. Venice is also a long way from Skopje in terms of differences apparent in the languages the inhabitants of the two cities speak, as well as in their ethnicities, nationalities, cultures, traditions and religious affiliations.

Most acknowledged biographers of Mother Teresa mention that she was Albanian but they refer to this fact very briefly, almost casually. So little is mentioned about her Albanian roots, parents, siblings, relatives and, indeed, about her eighteen years in Skopje that one has the impression that any information on this part of her life is hardly important. In many books, Mother Teresa's life from 1910 to 1928 is summed up in a very brief entry in the 'Important Dates'/'Date Chart'/'Chronological Table' appendix. This is then followed by another entry referring to the year 1928:

Apparently, these authors, and they are by no means the only ones, felt that nothing significant enough happened in Mother Teresa's life in Skopje from 1910 to 1928 to justify even a brief mention. As for those biographers who refer to her early years, in most cases they sum them up in one or two sentences and at most in one single paragraph. Malcolm Muggeridge, for instance, mentions only in passing Mother Teresa's early life and origin in *Something Beautiful for God*. So casual are his remarks about such seemingly 'irrelevant' biographical details throughout the book that one has the impression that he could have just as well ignored them completely. This is what he has to say in the *27 August 1910* entry in the 'Chronological Table' at the end of the book, before jumping to the next entry dated *29 November 1928*: [sic] *August 1910* Born of Albanian parents at Skopje, Yugoslavia. There were three children, one boy and two girls. She attended the government school.

Muggeridge's lack of interest in Mother Teresa's early years seems to have set a trend for the many books that appeared soon after the publi-cation of *Something Beautiful for God*. The following

Criticism of Mother Teresa 79

are some of the many similar sentences and paragraphs in later works regarding Mother Teresa's life from 1910 to 1928:

The daughter of an Albanian chemist, Agnes Gonxha Bojaxhiu was born on 27th [sic] August 1910 in Skopje, Yugoslavia.

27 [sic] *August 1910* Born Agnes Gonxha Bejaxhiu [sic], of Albanian parents at Skopje, Yugoslavia. There were three children, one boy and two girls. She attended the Government (Gimnaziya) school.

[Mother Teresa] was born on 27th [sic] August, 1910, in Skopje, Yugoslavia, of Albanian parents. Her name then was Agnes Gouxha [sic] Bojaxhiu. Her father was a grocer and Agnes was one of three children – two girls and a boy. She attended the local Government (Gimnazija) school...

Mother Teresa was born Agnes Gonxha Bojaxhiu in Skopje, Albania, on 26 August 1910, the youngest of three children. She had a comfort-able childhood – her father was a building contractor and importer, her mother was strict but loving with a deep faith. After her father's premature death, life became harder and to support her family Agnes' mother set up a business selling clothes and embroidery.

The quotes, which are more or less replicas of each other both in terms of the details they provide and their length, hardly justify John Cairns's claim that 'most of Mother Teresa's biographical details are now well known'. This may be true for Mother Teresa's life from September 1928, when she left Skopje, to the end of her life in September 1997 but this is certainly not the case for the 1910–1928 period.

To sum up the first eighteen years of a public figure of Mother Teresa's international standing in some few eclectic, rather picaresque, and inaccurate facts and figures like her father's professions (chemist, grocer, building contractor and importer), two different dates of birth (26 and 27 August), and several countries of birth (Albania, Macedonia, Serbia, Bosnia, Yugoslavia), is to oversimplify, if not vulgarize, the very notion of 'biography'. Some Mother Teresa biographers do refer very briefly to her childhood in Skopje.

80   *Mother Teresa*

Their interest in this early stage of her life, however, seems to be motivated mainly by their desire to highlight how deeply steeped in religion she was as a little girl as well as how devoutly Catholic her parents were, especially her mother. The exclusive attention and importance most Western and Indian biographers attach to Mother Teresa's religious background is such that one wonders if they would have chosen to refer at all to her early years if it were not for highlighting this specific aspect of her life in Skopje. To illustrate this point, here are again the same previously quoted sentences about her childhood, only this time I have also included the information about Mother Teresa's allegedly too religious childhood that follows immediately in each case:

The daughter of an Albanian chemist, Agnes Gonxha Bojaxhiu was born on 27th [sic] August 1910 in Skopje, Yugoslavia. As a young girl she was pious and well-behaved, and would have made someone a good wife, if at the age of twelve she had not become aware of another calling. Six years later some Jesuit fathers told her about the Sisters of Our Lady of Loreto in Calcutta. *And that was it!* (emphasis added)

[sic] *August 1910* Born Agnes Gonxha Bejaxhiu [sic], of Albanian parents at Skopje, Yugoslavia. There were three children, one boy and two girls. She attended the Government (Gimnaziya) school. While at school, she became a member of the Sodality. At that time, Yugoslav Jesuits had accepted to work in the Calcutta Archdiocese.

The first group arrived in Calcutta on 30 December 1925. One of them was sent to Kurseong. From there he sent enthusiastic letters about the Bengal Mission field. Those letters were read regularly to the Sodalists. Young Agnes was one of the Sodalists who volunteered for the Bengal Mission. She was put in touch with the Loreto nuns in Ireland as they were working in the Calcutta Archdiocese.

[Mother Teresa] was born on 27th [sic] August, 1910, in Skopje, Yugoslavia, of Albanian parents. Her name then was Agnes Gouxha [sic] Bojaxhiu. Her father was a grocer and Agnes was one of the three children – two girls and a boy. She attended the local Government (Gimnazija) school and whilst there became a member

Criticism of Mother Teresa 81

of a Catholic association for children known as the Sodality of Mary.

At the age of twelve, Agnes was already convinced that she had a vocation to the religious life. She was caught in a wave of enthusiasm for the missions and for the work of spreading the Gospel, an enthusiasm inspired by the writings of Pope Pius XI and endorsed by the insti-tution of the Feast of Christ the King. It was at this time that the Yugoslav Jesuits had agreed to work in the Calcutta Archdiocese and one of the first to arrive there was sent to Kurseong. From there he wrote fervent and inspiring letters about the work of the missionaries among the poor and the sick, and the child Agnes responded with the unshakeable conviction that her calling was to become a missionary.

Mother Teresa was born Agnes Gonxha Bojaxhiu in Skopje, Albania, on 26 August 1910, the youngest of three children. She had a comfort-able childhood – her father was a building contractor and importer, her mother was strict but loving with a deep faith. After her father's premature death, life became harder and to support her family Agnes' mother set up a business selling clothes and embroidery.

In her teens, Agnes became a member of a young people's group in her local parish called the Sodality and through the activities there, guided by a Jesuit priest, Agnes became interested in the world of missionaries.

It is true that Mother Teresa came from a religious background. Her father Nikollë was 'a faithful member of the Church'. He was close to several Catholic archbishops in Skopje and was always very generous to the church, even more so if he happened to like the local priest.

This was especially true in the case of the Albanian Archbishop Lazar Mjeda, who started working in Skopje in 1909. Several biographers of Mother Teresa have been keen to emphasize that Nikollë and the priest were close friends. Their friendship was the main reason why, to quote David Porter, Mother Teresa's father was 'even more generous towards the church than he would naturally have been'. Nikollë was 'a personal friend' of this particular priest, but their friendship was not motivated only by

82 *Mother Teresa*

the fact that they shared the Catholic faith. Lazar Mjeda was the brother of the promising Albanian classical poet Ndre Mjeda (1866–1937). As a young man, Ndre Mjeda had studied theology, rhetoric, Latin, Italian and literature in France, Spain, Croatia, Italy and Poland. It was as a student and later as a lecturer in music, philosophy, philology, logic and metaphysics in Italy and Poland during the 1880–1898 period that this talented writer wrote some of his best poetry, such as the poems 'The Nightingale's Lament' and 'Skanderbeg's Grave'. In these and other works, the poet expresses his love for Albania and how much he misses it in exile, and evokes the figure of the Albanian national hero.

As a token of appreciation for his generosity towards the church in Skopje, Lazar Mjeda gave Nikollë some 'good books', which included his brother's works. It is during this time that Agnes Gonxhe Bojaxhiu is known to have started enjoying reading poems written by Ndre Mjeda and other Albanian poets. Ndre Mjeda's nostalgic and patriotic work made a very strong impression especially on Nikollë who, like the poet, often travelled abroad and was strongly attached to his country. Nikollë was also something of an artist himself; he enjoyed singing and was an active member of a Skopje brass band. For a devoted patron of arts andan ardent Albanian patriot like Nikollë, it was only natural that he should express his wish to help financially not only Lazar Mjeda but also his brother Ndre. Nikollë's generosity left a lasting impression on the archbishop which is obvious from the way he expressed his gratitude to his affluent friend: 'May God reward you and your family in this life and in the afterlife for everything you have done for me, for the church and for the Albanian people.'

That Nikollë was far from a religious fanatic can also be seen from Mother Teresa's and her brother's recollections of him. The siblings would remember three things about their father: his generosity towards the poor, his gift as a story-teller, and his disciplinarian nature. None of these features appeared to have been motivated or influenced exclusively by his devotion to Catholicism. His generosity, for instance, was a mani festation of his humanitarian spirit for which he was well-known in his city. As a member of the Skopje City Council, he was in a unique

Criticism of Mother Teresa 83

position to know which religious and secular institutions, businesses and individuals needed financial support.

Being wealthy, Nikollë could, of course, afford to be more generous than his fellow Albanians (both Christians and Muslims) and citizens of other ethnicities and faiths. He became very popular in Skopje not only as a benefactor of the church but also for sponsoring important projects that improved significantly the city's cultural life and infrastructure. His popularity was enhanced especially as a result of his generosity towards the poor and the old who had either been abandoned by their own children or were forsaken by relatives and neighbours.

Nikollë was keen to instil in his three children feelings of respect and love for ordinary human beings. This is the reason why he and his wife often welcomed to their house poor people to whom they were not related, and introduce them to their children as 'relatives'. It was during these early years that Mother Teresa was taught not so much from the pulpit as around the family table that the poor, the vulnerable, the infirm and the dispossessed were not some 'human debris' to be kept at arm's length. Nikollë apparently wanted his children to learn to share their wealth with those who were not as fortunate as them. Mother Teresa never forgot his advice: 'My daughter, never take a morsel of food that you are not prepared to share with others.' Her brother Lazar would also always remember that, when he was little, his father would often give him instruc-tions to send parcels of money, clothes and food to the poor. Nikollë made sure that the poor who knocked on his door for help were not disappointed even when he was not at home. This is the reason why he left extra money with his wife when he was away on business.

Nikollë, the benefactor, was not a religious preacher. When he returned home from foreign trips he would always delight his children with stories. Neither Mother Teresa nor her brother, however, is known to have said anything about such memorable story-telling sessions being about religion or religious places abroad. Had Nikollë ever mentioned anything about any place of worship he had visited in countries like Italy and Egypt, where he is known to have travelled often, his children would have certainly

84   *Mother Teresa*

remembered such a thing, and if either Mother Teresa or Lazar had even slightly referred to his father's 'preaching' ability, this was certainly some-thing Mother Teresa's admiring biographers would have gladly recorded in their work.

The third facet of Nikollë's personality, his disciplinarian nature, was also not an expression of his religiosity. Mother Teresa's father was quite an advanced man for his time. Not only did he allow his two daughters to go to school, he was also keen that they should get the best education possible. Sensing perhaps a propensity for waywardness in his son, he would often reprimand him for not paying enough attention to his studies. In the evening he would usually go up to Lazar's room to ask him if he had behaved himself with friends and teachers and to test his knowledge of the subjects he was taking at school. Interestingly enough, Nikollë never seems to have advised his three children to behave themselves in a way that becomes a Catholic. More important for this disciplinarian but much-loved father, who always helped out the poor without drawing attention to himself, was that his children should never let him down. Being aware of how much he was respected in Skopje, he would often advise them to bear in mind his status, or as he used to put it: 'Never forget whose children you are.' While Mother Teresa's sympathetic biographers have failed to offer any strong evidence to prove what a strict religious father Nikollë was, they nearly always emphasize that her mother Drane was an exceptionally strict Catholic. I will discuss in detail in chapter five the extent to which reli-gion was important in Drane's life after she lost her husband and the impact her faith had on her children, especially on her youngest daughter Agnes. For the time being, suffice it to say that it appears that Drane was not any more religious than other Catholic Albanian women in Skopje throughout the time her husband was alive.

When Nikollë was alive Drane did not have his active social life, but nor was this wealthy woman cut off from the world. Being aware of how fortunate they were, she and her husband would often visit the church to express their gratitude to God for their prosperity. It would be wrong, however, to conclude, as many biographers have so far done, that Drane attended the church

Criticism of Mother Teresa

when her husband was alive simply because she was a devout adherent of the Catholic faith. In those days, the church was not only a place of worship but also an important venue for people to meet and attend activities which were not always of a strictly religious nature. The Bojaxhius' local church was well-known for organizing cultural events, especially concerts. For wealthy people like Drane and Nikollë, frequent visits to the parish church were also motivated by the wish to offer help to the needy. Church was the perfect venue for a generous couple like them to receive information about the people who needed support and how they could be reached. The church was also very important to Mother Teresa's parents in trying to achieve their aim of bringing up their children as responsible citizens. Drane and Nikollë took their three children to service regularly, and encouraged them to participate in charity events.

The Bojaxhius were also attached to the church because of music, which played an important role in their daily life. Like their father, the three children were passionate musicians. In the words of one of their childhood friends, Agnes in particular 'had real talent for music' and played the mandolin well. The church offered Agnes and her siblings a very good opportunity to pursue their musical talent. They were always active in the concerts and festivals organized by the church. Agnes and her sister were members of the church choir, and they were known as the 'two nightingales of the church', Agnes being the soprano and Age the contralto.

Nikollë and Drane were also keen for their children to go to church regularly because it was a place where they were taught by the clergy to take pride in their Albanian identity and the history of the Albanian nation. Local priests would often talk to the children about Albanian literature and the Albanian national hero Skanderbeg. It is also important to emphasize that both Nikollë and Drane taught the children by their own example how to be of help to those who were poor and vulnerable. Mother Teresa's parents were the first Samaritans she encountered in her life. Many years later when she wandered through the streets of Calcutta offering comfort to the old and the abandoned, she was hardly doing something new. As a little girl, she had regularly

86   *Mother Teresa*

accompanied her mother in similar charity missions through the streets of Skopje.

The charitable Mother Teresa was not born during the weeks she spent in the Irish convent in 1928, nor when she was first exposed to the shocking squalor of Colombo, Madras or Calcutta. The real genesis of the Mother Teresa many people in Calcutta, across India and throughout the world came to know and admire in the second half of the twentieth century is found in the little and unpretentious Balkan town of Skopje. Being brought up by devoted, demanding and open-minded parents, listening to the preaching of several devout Albanian and Slavic Catholic priests, enjoying the company of Albanian, Croat, Slovene, Hungarian, Italian and Jewish friends, growing up in a thriving multi-ethnic, multi-religious and multi-cultural community – the Bojaxhiu children obviously had a very healthy beginning in life. This kind of childhood was bound to have a positive impact on them, especially on the more sensitive Agnes.

The tolerant views and attitudes towards people of different ethnicities and religions she displayed as a nun and as a charity worker were sown during her early years in Skopje. Georges Gorrée and Jean Barbier's conclu-sion that once 'some Jesuit fathers told her about the Sisters of Our Lady of Loretto in Calcutta. And that was it, is rather hasty and simplistic, and as such misleading. There was no 'And that was it!' in Mother Teresa's life. An interpretation like this ignores, belittles and trivializes the huge impact her family, the local church and a multi-culturally diverse city like Skopje had on Mother Teresa throughout the 1910–1928 period and beyond. Mother Teresa's decision to become a nun was not taken suddenly and certainly not in a hurry. Exceptional individuals like her do not embark on a life mission on a sudden impulse.

The huge formative impact her background had on Mother Teresa has been largely ignored or is mentioned only in passing in the vast literature on her intended mainly for Western and middle-class Indian readers. Up until the mid-1980s not many people in India and the West knew much about Mother Teresa's ethnic, cultural and national roots. From then onwards, details

Criticism of Mother Teresa

about her early life began to appear in some texts. In most cases, however, this flimsy information is presented more in the form of parables about a legendary figure who seemed to have lived and worked in a very distant, almost mythological past, than as well-researched biographical details about the life of one of the most influential twentieth-century figures.

So far, biographers of Mother Teresa refer to the city of Skopje mainly to highlight its exotic nature, or to introduce readers to some equally exotic and 'primitive' aspects of Mother Teresa's fellow countrymen like *besa* (Albanian for 'promise/word of honour'), and the 'blood feud', which to this day remain some of the most preferred themes for most Western writers and researchers interested in Albania and the Balkans. In a half-hearted and unsuccessful attempt to find some explan-ation for Mother Teresa's devotion to Christ in the essentially 'folkloric' nature of her people, Eileen Egan is keen to highlight in the opening chapter 'The Strands of Life' of her 1986 biography that 'ineradicable aspect of Albanian identity deeply imbedded in her character. It throws a vivid light on the reality of a rare woman.' This aspect is, of course, *besa*, to which Egan returns in the second chapter 'The Call Within a Call':

It is a concept deep in the consciousness of Albanians that refers to the absolute sacredness of the word of honor, the inviolability of the pledged word in daily life. The concept... is contained in the word *besa*.

As Mother Teresa explained it to me, should a family promise hospi tality to someone and he came to claim it, the family would provide it and protect that person at any cost. The cost might be heavy indeed if the person claiming hospitality were, as often happened, a hunted man stalked by seekers after retribution or vengeance. The pledge would be fulfilled even in the extreme situation that word came that the guest had been involved in the death of a member of the host family. As she was explaining *besa*, one could transport oneself back to the beleaguered people of Albania, engaged not only in resistance to occupation, but also in feuds among themselves. Their very lives depended on no document, no treaty, but hung by the slender thread of a simple word of honor.

88   *Mother Teresa*

Egan does not make it clear if she asked Mother Teresa about the concept of *besa* or if the nun had initiated the discussion herself. Albanians often like to talk to foreigners about their ancient national virtue of *besa* and their proverbial hospitality, especially to those foreigners with a special interest in the exotic. It would not be surprising if Mother Teresa preferred to talk to her Western biographers about Albanian ancient customs. There are indications that, at least in private, she took pride in her Albanian 1 roots, and would often talk about her nation's virtues. And not necessarily only to her Western friends with an eye for the exotic. She appears to have also talked about Albanian traditions, especially the concept of *besa*, to her fellow nuns. One of the questions asked by Mother Teresa's sisters attending my lectures at St Xavier's College in Calcutta on 1 July 2005 was about the significance of *besa* in the context of Mother Teresa's devotion to Jesus.

No matter how much or how little Mother Teresa liked to talk to her Western friends and fellow sisters about *besa*, it would be naïve and inac curate to try to interpret her attachment to Christ exclusively or mainly in the light of the ancient Albanian custom of honouring a pledge. It is true that Mother Teresa's devotion to the Catholic faith is a modern example of the determination on the part of some of her fellow Albanians to adhere to Christianity. On the other hand, Mother Teresa's lifetime attachment to Jesus can be best explained not so much in the context of an exotic national custom or tradition such as *besa*, but of a complex set of personal circumstances.

Fanciful and exotic theories and explanations as to how and why an Albanian girl chose to become a nun are unlikely to satisfy those who admire Mother Teresa but do not necessarily share her faith, or any faith for that matter. The importance that Egan attaches to the Albanian concept of *besa* to explore and explain the unique nature of Mother Teresa's bond with Jesus is misleading and not very useful even for those followers of Catholicism whose admiration for Mother Teresadoesn ots topt hemf roms earching for a rational explanation for her initial attachment and lifetime devotion to Jesus. Egan's attempts to explain the 'unexplainable' are also disappointing because her references to *besa* are inconsequential in the context in which the term crops up in her

Criticism of Mother Teresa 89

1986 biography. Such haphazard references indicate once again how superficially Mother Teresa's background and her years in Skopje have been treated even by some of her best-known biographers and friends. Fantasy and speculation have not always served Mother Teresa experts well, espe-cially those who have been and still remain indifferent to her Skopje years. A full-length study of the nun's early life has still to be written, and if such a work could be penned by a dispassionate scholar, it could prove very useful in understanding and reinterpreting some key aspects of Mother Teresa's faith and journey from 1928 when she left Skopje for Ireland and then for India. A biography of Agnes Gonxhe Bojaxhiu's life in Skopje would be an enlightening introduction to the life of the nun Mother Teresa.

MOTHER TERESA IN THE REPUBLIC OF MACEDONIA

Memorial Museum

The Memorial House of Mother Teresa was opened in Mother Teresa's hometown of Skopje, present-day Republic of Macedonia (41.993827°N 21.430689°E). The museum has a significant selection of objects from Mother Teresa's life in Skopje and relics from her later life. In the memorial room there is a model of her family home, made by Vojo Georgievski. Next to the memorial room, there is an area with the image of Mother Teresa as well as a memorial park and fountain.

Memorial plaque

Just at the edge of Skopje's City Mall (Gradski Trgovski Centar), is the place where the house of Mother Teresa used to stand. The memorial plaque was dedicated in March 1998 and it reads: "On this place was the house where Gond•a Bojad•iu - Mother Teresa - born on 26 August 1910". Her message to the world is also inscribed: "The world is not hungry for bread, but for love."

Mother Teresa in Kosovo

Mother Teresa is held in high regard among Kosovars, who consider her one of their own, as she spent her childhood in

90 *Mother Teresa*

Kosovo. The main street in Kosovo's capital Pristina is called Mother Teresa Street *(Rruga Nëna Terezë)*. Zana Krasniqi, the Miss Kosovo Universe 2008, made mention of Mother Teresa, calling her a great ancestor.

Mother Teresa in India

- In 1991, the Senate of Serampore College, Serampore, West Bengal, conferred upon her the degree of Doctor of Divinity (D.D.),*honoris causa*.
- The historic "Park Street" of Calcutta was renamed to "Mother Teresa Sarani".
- Indian Railways introduced a new train, "Mother Express", named after Mother Teresa, on August 26, 2010, to mark her birth centenary. The coaches of the train will be painted blue, the trademark border of the habit worn by the order she founded. This train will connect important destinations in the country.
- Tamil Nadu State government organised centenary celebrations of Mother Teresa on December 4, 2010, in Chennai headed by Tamil Nadu chief minister M Karunanidhi.

Musical Tribute

- In 1998, a musical tribute album was compiled and released by Lion Communications (Polygram Records). The album featured artists from around the world paying tribute to Mother Teresa and was called "Mother, We'll Miss You". Some of the artists included on the CD were Jose Feliciano and gospel group Walt Whitman and the Soul Children of Chicago. The album was produced by Scottish singer Dave Kelly, who also wrote and performed the title track. Over fifty major American newspapers, such as theBoston Globe and the Philadelphia Inquirer, featured stories on the release of the tribute album and also took this opportunity to honor the life and work of Mother Teresa.

Legacy of Mother Teresa

In appearance Mother Teresa was both tiny and energetic. Her face was quite wrinkled, but her dark eyes commanded attention, radiating an energy and intelligence that shone without expressing nervousness or impatience.

Conservatives within the Catholic Church sometimes used her as a symbol of traditional religious values that they felt were lacking in their churches.

By most accounts she was a saint for the times, and several almost adoring books and articles started to canonize (declare a saint) her in the 1980s and well into the 1990s. She herself tried to deflect all attention away from what she did to either the works of her group or to the God who was her inspiration.

The Missionaries of Charity, who had brothers as well as sisters by the mid-1980s, are guided by the constitution Mother Teresa wrote for them.

They have their vivid memo ries of the love for the poor that created the phenomenon of Mother Teresa in the first place. The final part of her story will be the lasting impact her memory has on the next generations of missionaries, as well as on the world as a whole.

EARLY LIFE

Mother Teresa of Calcutta was born Agnes Gonxha Bojaxhiu in Skopje, Macedonia, on August 27, 1910. At the time of her birth Skopje was located within the Ottoman Empire, a vast empire controlled by the Turks in the fifteenth and sixteenth centuries. Agnes was the last of three children born to Nikola and Dranafile Bojaxhiu, Albanian grocers.

When Agnes was nine years old, her happy, comfortable, close-knit family life was upset when her father died. She attended

92 *Mother Teresa*

public school in Skopje, and first showed religious interests as a member of a school society that focused on foreign missions (groups that travel to foreign countries to spread their religious beliefs). By the age of twelve she felt she had a calling to help the poor.

This calling took sharper focus through Mother Teresa's teenage years,w hens hew ases peciallyi nspiredb yr eportso fw orkb eing done in India by Yugoslav Jesuit missionaries serving in Bengal, India.

When she was eighteen, Mother Teresa left home to join a community of Irish nuns, the Sisters of Loretto, who had a mission in Calcutta, India. She received training in Dublin, Ireland, and in Darjeeling, India, taking her first religious vows in 1928 and her final religious vows in 1937.

One of Mother Teresa's first assignments was to teach, and eventually to serve as principal, in a girls' high school in Calcutta. Although the school was close to the slums (terribly poor sections), the students were mainly wealthy. In 1946 Mother Teresa experienced what she called a second vocation or "call within a call." She felt an inner urging to leave the convent life (life of a nun) and work directly with the poor. In 1948 the Vatican (residence of the pope in Vatican City, Italy) gave her permission to leave the Sisters of Loretto and to start a new work under the guidance of the Archbishop of Calcutta.

Founding the Missionaries of Charity

To prepare to work with the poor, Mother Teresa took an intensive medical training with the American Medical Missionary Sisters in Patna, India. Her first venture in Calcutta was to gather unschooled children from the slums and start to teach them. She quickly attracted both financial support and volunteers. In 1950 her group, now called the Missionaries of Charity, received official status as a religious community within the Archdiocese of Calcutta. Members took the traditional vows of poverty, chastity (purity), and obedience, but they added a fourth vow — to give free service to the most poor.

The Missionaries of Charity received considerable publicity, and Mother Teresa used it to benefit her work. In 1957 they began

Legacy of Mother Teresa

to work with lepers (those suffering from leprosy, a terrible infectious disease) and slowly expanded their educational work, at one point running nine elementary schools in Calcutta. They also opened a home for orphans and abandoned children. Before long they had a presence in more than twenty-two Indian cities. Mother Teresa also visited other countries such as Ceylon (now Sri Lanka), Australia, Tanzania, Venezuela, and Italy to begin new foundations.

Mother Teresa's Legacy

"The very fact that God has placed a certain soul in your way is a sign that God wants you to do something for them," Mother Teresa said. Her order, The Missionaries of Charity, was founded on this truth. I am one of those who can testify to its power.

I had the privilege of meeting Mother Teresa in 1985 when she was in Washington for the opening of one of her homes. I had some vague notion of helping her raise money for her work. To my surprise she didn't seem at all interested in what I could do for her. Without exaggeration, I can say that one meeting changed my life.

But my contact with Mother Teresa was incidental compared to that of Bob Macauley, founder of AmeriCares. Bob worked with her on many occasions.

On one of these occasions a few years before she died, Bob was on a plane with her on the way to visit one of her homes in South America. They were seated side by side in the coach section of a regional jet, this powerful, but small lady and a massive man — Bob was 6' 4" — with about 100 other passengers.

Shortly after the flight took off, the cabin attendants began meal service. When the attendant came to Mother Teresa she held up her hand.

"How much does this meal cost?" she asked.

The attendant said she didn't know exactly, but probably about $5 American.

Mother said, "If I don't eat the meal, can I have the $5 for the poor?"

94   *Mother Teresa*

The attendant did not know how to respond. She said she would have to ask someone. Dutifully, she went forward and reported Mother Teresa's request to the pilot who then contacted the company representative on the ground.

In a few minutes, the attendant returned with the happy news. "Yes, Mother, you may have the money for the poor."

Mother Teresa smiled and returned her tray. Bob immediately followed her example and handed his tray back, as well. In short order, everyone on the plane followed suit.

"I thought we had done pretty well," Bob said, "until we got off the plane. Then Mother Teresa turned to me and said, "Get the food, Bob."

When Bob asked her what she meant, she said, "The airline can't use it now. Get the food and we will take it to the poor."

Bob found the airline's representative and repeated Mother Teresa's request. In a few minutes, he returned with the news they had agreed to let her have the unused food as well.

"Now get the trucks, Bob," Mother Teresa said.

When he looked puzzled, she explained, "We can't deliver the food without trucks. Ask if we can use their trucks to deliver the food to the poor."

Bob often told this story to illustrate how focused and relentless Mother was in her service to the poor. "We create poverty," she said, "because we will not share."

"The greatest challenge of the day," Dorothy Day wrote, "is how to bring about a revolution of the heart, a revolution which has to start with each one of us." Mother Teresa understood that challenge and sought in her quiet way to spark that effort.

There can only be one Mother Teresa, but her truth speaks to us all. God has given each of us the capacity to achieve some end necessary to others. Each of us has the power to increase the sum of the world's happiness.

Every little deed counts. Peace begins with a smile. Salvation can be found in the simple act of extending a hand. The humblest among us can, by shear act of will, help create heaven on earth.

Legacy of Mother Teresa 95

MOTHER TERESA'S TROUBLED LEGACY

I was in the Mother Teresa-themed gift shop located beside – but bearing no official relationship to – the Missionaries of Charity headquarters on AJC Bose Road in Kolkata. My two months of volunteering had concluded and I was shopping for a gift for my Catholic grandmother.

Though intended rhetorically, the woman's words begged the question that I had been pondering for weeks: what value sacredness?

Missionaries of Charity exemplifies the danger of inviolability. Established by Mother Teresa in 1950, it consists of over 4,500 Catholic nuns in 133 countries. While the Catholic Church continues to deflect an onslaught of criticism for its mandates, few are willing to challenge the charity founded by the world's favourite Sister.

But there is mounting evidence against Missionaries of Charity, from a gross mismanagement ofFUNDS to a fundamentalist doctrine that justifies the unnecessary suffering of the very individuals the organization claims to be helping.

In the article 'Mother Teresa: Where Are Her Millions?', Stern magazine reported that Missionaries of Charity receives an estimated $100 million in annual revenue. In the same article, former Missionaries of Charity nun Susan Shields stated that her order in the Bronx regularly accepts cheques for upwards of $50,000.

And yet, despite all appearances of being a lucrative charity, I discovered that the resources and care provided at one of its best-known facilities are horrifically and disproportionately negligible.

Judge not?

I arrived in Kolkata shortly after Diwali, when strings of lights cascading down the sides of buildings twinkled above the sleeping street children.

I was assigned a placement at Kalighat: Mother Teresa's home for the dying, and the first Missionaries of Charity site. Since the building was undergoing renovations, the residents were temporarily relocated to a wing in the long-term care facility Prem Dan.

The dark, concrete dormitories in Prem Dan had rows of army-style cots lining the walls. The squat-style toilets were in a narrow room slick with water, urine and faeces. Patients wearing foot bandages soon found their dressings soaking and rank, and those unable to walk upright were forced – through a scarcity of wheelchairs and crutches – to crawl through the mess in order to relieve themselves.

Judge not lest ye be judged, I imagined my grandmother lecturing.

And while I had abandoned all pretence of religion years ago, it was still practical advice. So I turned my attention to my primary task as a volunteer: laundry. Perhaps naively, I assumed that it would allow me to make a difference while working in a sanitary environment. These illusions were dispelled the moment I saw the cramped room with concrete walls and a drain at one end.

The washing process began when a nun dropped the freshly soiled clothing onto the floor by the drain and brushed the largest chunks of human waste down the hole with a broom. Another nun dunked the garment in disinfectant and passed it off to a volunteer, who scrubbed it in soapy water.

From there, the article was passed through two rinsing basins before being wrung out and carried to a clothesline on the roof.

This was a direly insufficient method of sanitization that posed a health risk to residents and volunteers alike.

This was a direly insufficient method of sanitization that posed a health risk to residents and volunteers alike.

'Seven volunteers have come down with fevers in the last month. Four were even hospitalized,' said the young bearded Frenchman stationed at the basin beside me. 'Make sure you wash your hands before you eat lunch.'

When I asked why there was no washing machine, he referred to the vows of the Missionaries of Charity congregation: chastity, poverty and obedience.

Legacy of Mother Teresa 97

Adjacent to the laundry room was the surgery. Medical procedures were performed by a nun and an Italian nurse. However, soon after I arrived, the latter fell so ill that she was forced to fly home. This left the surgery desperately short-handed. As a former lifeguard with basic first-aid training, I offered my services.

Those admitted with severe lesions had maggots writhing among the rotten skin. The patients were predominantly homeless and, without the protection of bandages, flies had laid eggs in their lacerations.

One woman bore over 50 finger-sized holes in her scalp, and we spent more than an hour nipping at the larvae with our tweezers as she screamed in agony.

It required five more days of plucking to cease the infestation. As Sister C scrubbed and hacked away at another patient's infections, I administered topical saline solution and iodine.

A handful of male volunteers restrained patients who were sobbing and howling for their gods and their mothers.

'Aren't you giving them morphine?' I asked.

The nun vehemently shook her head. 'No. Only Diclofenac.'

Diclofenac is an analgesic painkiller commonly used to treat arthritis and gout.

It is not an anaesthetic and does not eliminate sensation. Yet this was Sister C's treatment of choice for patients undergoing severe pain – despite the fact that directly across the hall was a room brimming with supplies provided by Catholic hospitals around the world. Local anaesthetic is often one of the first items donated.

Sister C's rationale, however, can be summed up by a statement made by Mother Teresa at a Washington press conference shortly before her death in 1997: 'I think it is very beautiful for the poor to accept their lot, to share it with the passion of Christ. I think the world is being much helped by the suffering of the poor people.' This clearly indicates that Mother Teresa and, by extension, Missionaries of Charity believe that suffering enhances holiness.

Serving her religion

After all, it was Mother Teresa's primary intention to serve her religion – helping others was merely the means of doing so. 'There is always the danger that we may become only social workers... Our works are only an expression of our love for Christ,' she once told journalist Malcolm Muggeridge.

Back in the surgery, pain management was not the only area of grave concern – the hygiene standard was comparable to that in the laundry.

There were no paper sheets on the examination table (I wiped it down with disinfectant at the end of each day), leading to an astronomical risk of cross-contamination.

This was especially dangerous since many of the patients suffered from HIV/AIDS, hepatitis C, typhoid and tuberculosis. The only gloves available to me were extra large, so I purchased my own at the localMARKET. Sister C worked bare-handed – and didn't always wash between patients.

The poor maintenance of the surgery was largely due to the fact that Sister C was the only nun trained as a nurse, and was therefore extremely busy. Occasionally she had to enlist the assistance of nuns with few or no medical skills. I witnessed a giggling novice nun attempt to administer an injection while the patient shrieked in fear and pain.

These were only a few of the many instances of the negligence I encountered at Kalighat. I learned from other volunteers that similar incidents were occurring at Missionaries of Charity homes across the city.

Over the years, *Forbes India*, Britain's Channel 4 TV and journalist Christopher Hitchens have all investigated the millions of dollars unaccounted for by Missionaries of Charity.

But their reports have not been enough to spur public action: awareness can only go so far against the idea of the consecrated. It is only by removing the concept of inviolability that we will be able to face the objective truth of abuse and neglect. Only then will the Missionaries of Charity finally be held accountable for its actions.

Legacy of Mother T eresa 99

DEDICATION TO THE VERY POOR

Mother Teresa's group continued to expand throughout the 1970s, opening new missions in places such as Amman, Jordan; London, England; and New York, New York.

She received both recognition and financial support through such awards as the Pope John XXIII Peace Prize and a grant from the Joseph Kennedy Jr.Foundation. Benefactors, or those donating money, regularly would arrive to support works in progress or to encourage the Sisters to open new ventures.

By 1979 Mother Teresa's groups had more than two hundred different operations in over twenty-five countries around the world, with dozens more ventures on the horizon.

The same year she was awarded the Nobel Prize for Peace. In 1986 she persuaded President Fidel Castro (1926–) to allow a mission in Cuba.

The characteristics of all of Mother Teresa's works—shelters for the dying, orphanages, and homes for the mentally ill— continued to be of service to the very poor.

In 1988 Mother Teresa sent her Missionaries of Charity into Russia and opened a home for acquired immune deficiency syndrome (AIDS; an incurable disease that weakens the immune system) patients in San Francisco, California. In 1991 she returned home to Albania and opened a home in Tirana, the capital. At this time there were 168 homes operating in India.

THE LEGACY OF LOVE OF BLESSED MOTHER TERESA

Agnes Gonxhe Bojaxhiu was initially called to religious life with the Sisters of Loreto. Taking the name of Sister Teresa, this young Albanian woman was sent to India in 1929 after first learning English in Ireland.

It was not until she had been teaching at a school for girls in Calcutta for 15 years that she received her "calling within a calling" – a summons to serve the poor, living among them. By then she was called Mother Teresa, having taken her final vows several

100   *Mother Teresa*

years before. However, because this was not part of the mission of the Sisters of Loreto, a teaching order, nearly two years passed before she was given permission to begin what she saw as her work.

In 1948, she put on her famous white and blue sari for the first time and entered the world of the poor.

Each day Mother Teresa went out, rosary in hand, to find and nurse the sick and dying who were lying in the streets, wash the sores of the diseased, and care for the orphaned.

She called it the Gospel on five fingers – *You did it to me.* "'Whatsoever you do to the least of my brothers, that you do unto me'; for I was hungry, thirsty, naked, homeless, unwanted, untouchable – and *you did it to me*" (cf. Matthew 25:34-40).

Soon, students from the Loreto school were helping her in the streets of Calcutta and, in 1950, a new congregation was established, the Missionaries of Charity.

Mother Teresa and her sisters were driven, she explained, by the desire to quench the thirst of Jesus on the Cross for love (John 19:28).

Their aim was, and is, to see and care for Jesus in the poor, most especially the poorest of the poor, that is, the unwanted, unloved, forgotten, abandoned, and uncared for throughout society.

"Let us not make a mistake," she said, "that the hunger is only for a piece of bread. The hunger of today is much greater: for love – to be wanted, to be loved, to be cared for, to be somebody." Today, there are Missionaries of Charity serving all around the world, including their Gift of Peace Convent, which has served the homeless and terminally ill here in Washington for 27 years.

Upon her beatification, six years after her death in 1997, Blessed Pope John Paul II said that Mother Teresa "wanted to be a sign of 'God's love, God's presence and God's compassion,' and so remind all of the value and dignity of each of God's children, 'created to love and be loved.'"

This is the legacy that she leaves us. Having had the privilege of meeting and praying with Mother Teresa and visiting some of

Legacy of Mother Teresa

the centers of the Missionaries of Charity, I thank God for the grace given to the world in her. What a witness for us all to emulate.

Blessed Mother Teresa exhorts us to be missionaries of love, "You are God's love in action. Through you, God is still loving the world. Each time people come into contact with us, they must become different and better people because of having met us. We must radiate God's love."

This is how his kingdom is built up. Following her namesake in religion, Saint Thérèse of Lisieux, Mother Teresa teaches that this does not require big things, but doing small things with great love. We do this one day at a time, one person at a time, but without delay, she reminds us.

"Our work is for today, yesterday has gone, tomorrow has not yet come – today, we have only today to make Jesus known, loved, served, fed, clothed, sheltered, etc. Today – do not to wait for tomorrow. Tomorrow might not come. Tomorrow we will not have them if we do not feed them today."

Saint Teresa

Despite the appeal of this saintly work, all commentators remarked that Mother Teresa herself was the most important reason for the growth of her order and the fame that came to it. Unlike many "social critics," she did not find it necessary to attack the economic or political structures of the cultures that were producing the terribly poor people she was serving. For her, the primary rule was a constant love, and when social critics or religious reformers (improvers) chose to demonstrate anger at the evils of structures underlying poverty and suffering, that was between them and God.

In the 1980s and 1990s Mother Teresa's health problems became a concern. She suffered a heart attack while visiting Pope John Paul II (1920–) in 1983. She had a near fatal heart attack in 1989 and began wearing a pacemaker, a device that regulates the heartbeat.

In March 1997, after an eight week selection process, sixty-three-year-old Sister Nirmala was named as the new leader of the

102 *Mother Teresa*

Missionaries of Charity. Although Mother Teresa had been trying to cut back on her duties for some time because of her health, she stayed on in an advisory role to Sister Nirmala.

Mother Teresa celebrated her eighty-seventh birthday in August, and died shortly thereafter of a heart attack on September 5, 1997. The world grieved her loss and one mourner noted, "It was Mother herself who poor people respected. When they bury her, we will have lost something that cannot be replaced."

5 Mother Teresa in Calcutta

"By blood, I am Albanian. By citizenship, an Indian. By faith, I am a Catholic nun. As to my calling, I belong to the world. As to my heart, I belong entirely to the Heart of Jesus. "Small of stature, rocklike in faith, Mother Teresa of Calcutta was entrusted with the mission of proclaiming God's thirsting love for humanity, especially for the poorest of the poor. *"God still loves the world and He sends you and me to be His love and His compassion to the poor."* S he was a soul filled with the light of Christ, on fire with love for Him and burning with one desire: *"to quench His thirst for love and for souls."*

This luminous messenger of God's love was born on 26 August 1910 in Skopje, a city situated at the crossroads of Balkan history. The youngest of the children born to Nikola and Drane Bojaxhiu, she was baptised Gonxha Agnes, received her First Communion at the age of five and a half and was confirmed in November 1916. From the day of her First Holy Communion, a love for souls was within her. Her father's sudden death when Gonxha was about eight years old left in the family in financial straits. Drane raised her children firmly and lovingly, greatly influencing her daughter's character and vocation. Gonxha's religious formation was further assisted by the vibrant Jesuit parish of the Sacred Heart in which she was much involved.

At the age of eighteen, moved by a desire to become a missionary, Gonxha left her home in September 1928 to join the Institute of the Blessed Virgin Mary, known as the Sisters of Loreto, in Ireland. There she received the name Sister Mary Teresa after St. Thérèse of Lisieux. In December, she departed for India, arriving in Calcutta on 6 January 1929. After making her First Profession of Vows in May 1931, Sister Teresa was assigned to the Loreto Entally community in Calcutta and taught at St. Mary's School for girls. On 24 May 1937, Sister Teresa made her Final

104   *Mother Teresa*

Profession of Vows, becoming, as she said, the *"spouse of Jesus"* for *"all eternity."* From that time on she was called Mother Teresa. She continued teaching at St. Mary's and in 1944 became the school's principal. A person of profound prayer and deep love for her religious sisters and her students, Mother Teresa's twenty years in Loreto were filled with profound happiness. Noted for her charity, unselfishness and courage, her capacity for hard work and a natural talent for organization, she lived out her consecration to Jesus, in the midst of her companions, with fidelity and joy.

On 10 September 1946 during the train ride from Calcutta to Darjeeling for her annual retreat, Mother Teresa received her *"inspiration,"*h er *"call within a call."* On that day, in a way she would never explain, Jesus' thirst for love and for souls took hold of her heart and the desire to satiate His thirst became the driving force of her life. Over the course of the next weeks and months, by means of interior locutions and visions, Jesus revealed to her the desire of His heart for *"victims of love"* who would *"radiate His love on souls." "Come be My light,"* He begged her. *"I cannot go alone."* He revealed His pain at the neglect of the poor, His sorrow at their ignorance of Him and His longing for their love. He asked Mother Teresa to establish a religious community, Missionaries of Charity, dedicated to the service of the poorest of the poor. Nearly two years of testing and discernment passed before Mother Teresa received permission to begin. On August 17, 1948, she dressed for the first time in a white, blue-bordered sari and passed through the gates of her beloved Loreto convent to enter the world of the poor.

After a short course with the Medical Mission Sisters in Patna, Mother Teresa returned to Calcutta and found temporary lodging with the Little Sisters of the Poor. On 21 December she went for the first time to the slums. She visited families, washed the sores of some children, cared for an old man lying sick on the road and nursed a woman dying of hunger and TB. She started each day in communion with Jesus in the Eucharist and then went out, rosary in her hand, to find and serve Him in *"the unwanted, the unloved, the uncared for."*After some months, she was joined, one by one, by her former students.

Mother Teresa in Calcutta 105

On 7 October 1950 the new congregation of the Missionaries of Charity was officially established in the Archdiocese of Calcutta. By the early 1960s, Mother Teresa began to send her Sisters to other parts of India. The Decree of Praise granted to the Congregation by Pope Paul VI in February 1965 encouraged her to open a house in Venezuela. It was soon followed by foundations in Rome and Tanzania and, eventually, on every continent. Starting in 1980 and continuing through the 1990s, Mother Teresa opened houses in almost all of the communist countries, including the former Soviet Union, Albania and Cuba.

In order to respond better to both the physical and spiritual needs of the poor, Mother Teresa founded the *Missionaries of Charity Brothers* in 1963, in 1976 the *contemplative branch* of the Sisters, in 1979 the *Contemplative Brothers*, and in 1984 the *Missionaries of Charity Fathers*. Yet her inspiration was not limited to those with religious vocations. She formed the *Co-Workers of Mother Teresa* and the *Sick and Suffering Co-Workers,* people of many faiths and nationalities with whom she shared her spirit of prayer, simplicity, sacrifice and her apostolate of humble works of love. This spirit later inspired the *Lay Missionaries of Charity.* In answer to the requests of many priests, in 1981 Mother Teresa also began the *Corpus Christi Movement for Priests* as a *"little way of holiness"* f or those who desire to share in her charism and spirit.

During the years of rapid growth the world began to turn its eyes towards Mother Teresa and the work she had started. Numerous awards, beginning with the Indian Padmashri Award in 1962 and notably the Nobel Peace Prize in 1979, honoured her work, while an increasingly interested media began to follow her activities. She received both prizes and attention *"for the glory of God and in the name of the poor."*

The whole of Mother Teresa's life and labour bore witness to the joy of loving, the greatness and dignity of every human person, the value of little things done faithfully and with love, and the surpassing worth of friendship with God. But there was another heroic side of this great woman that was revealed only after her death. Hidden from all eyes, hidden even from those closest to her, was her interior life marked by an experience of a deep,

106 *Mother Teresa*

painful and abiding feeling of being separated from God, even rejected by Him, along with an ever-increasing longing for His love. She called her inner experience, *"the darkness."* The "painful night" of her soul, which began around the time she started her work for the poor and continued to the end of her life, led Mother Teresa to an ever more profound union with God. Through the darkness she mystically participated in the thirst of Jesus, in His painful and burning longing for love, and she shared in the interior desolation of the poor.

During the last years of her life, despite increasingly severe health problems, Mother Teresa continued to govern her Society and respond to the needs of the poor and the Church. By 1997, Mother Teresa's Sisters numbered nearly 4,000 members and were established in 610 foundations in 123 countries of the world. In March 1997 she blessed her newly-elected successor as Superior General of the Missionaries of Charity and then made one more trip abroad. After meeting Pope John Paul II for the last time, she returned to Calcutta and spent her final weeks receiving visitors and instructing her Sisters. On 5 September Mother Teresa's earthly life came to an end. She was given the honour of a state funeral by the Government of India and her body was buried in the Mother House of the Missionaries of Charity. Her tomb quickly became a place of pilgrimage and prayer for people of all faiths, rich and poor alike. Mother Teresa left a testament of unshakable faith, invincible hope and extraordinary charity. Her response to Jesus' plea, "Come be My light," made her a Missionary of Charity, a "mother to the poor," a symbol of compassion to the world, and a living witness to the thirsting love of God.

Less than two years after her death, in view of Mother Teresa's widespread reputation of holiness and the favours being reported, Pope John Paul II permitted the opening of her Cause of Canonization. On 20 December 2002 he approved the decrees of her heroic virtues and miracles.

CALLED TO RELIGIOUS LIFE

At 18, Gonxha decided to follow the path that seems to have been unconsciously unfolding throughout her life. She chose the

Mother Teresa in Calcutt a 107

Loreto Sisters of Dublin, missionaries and educators founded in the 17th century to educate young girls.

In 1928, the future Mother Teresa began her religious life in Ireland, far from her family and the life she'd known, never seeing her mother again in this life, speaking a language few understood. During this period a sister novice remembered her as "very small, quiet and shy," and another member of the congregation described her as "ordinary."

Mother Teresa herself, even with the later decision to begin her own community of religious, continued to value her beginnings with the Loreto sisters and to maintain close ties. Unwavering commitment and self-discipline, always a part of her life and reinforced in her association with the Loreto sisters, seemed to stay with her throughout her life.

One year later, in 1929, Gonxha was sent to Darjeeling to the novitiate of the Sisters of Loreto. In 1931, she made her first vows there, choosing the name of Teresa, honoring both saints of the same name, Teresa of Avila and Therese of Lisieux. In keeping with the usual procedures of the congregation and her deepest desires, it was time for the new Sister Teresa to begin her years of service to God's people. She was sent to St. Mary's, a high school for girls in a district of Calcutta.

Here she began a career teaching history and geography, which she reportedly did with dedication and enjoyment for the next 15 years. It was in the protected environment of this school for the daughters of the wealthy that Teresa's new "vocation" developed and grew. This was the clear message, the invitation to her "second calling," that Teresa heard on that fateful day in 1946 when she traveled to Darjeeling for retreat.

The Streets of Calcutta

During the next two years, Teresa pursued every avenue to follow what she "never doubted" was the direction God was pointing her. She was "to give up even Loreto where I was very happy and to go out in the streets. I heard the call to give up all and follow Christ into the slums to serve him among the poorest of the poor."

108   *Mother Teresa*

Technicalities and practicalities abounded. She had to be released formally, not from her perpetual vows, but from living within the convents of the Sisters of Loreto.

She had to confront the Church's resistance to forming new religious communities, and receive permission from the Archbishop of Calcutta to serve the poor openly on the streets.

She had to figure out how to live and work on the streets, without the safety and comfort of the convent. As for clothing, Teresa decided she would set aside the habit she had worn during her years as a Loreto sister and wear the ordinary dress of an Indian woman: a plain white sari and sandals.

Teresa first went to Patna for a few months to prepare for her future work by taking a nursing course. In 1948 she received permission from Pius XII to leave her community and live as an independent nun. So back to Calcutta she went and found a small hovel to rent to begin her new undertaking.

Wisely, she thought to start by teaching the children of the slums, an endeavor she knew well. Though she had no proper equipment, she made use of what was available — writing in the dirt. She strove to make the children of the poor literate, to teach them basic hygiene. As they grew to know her, she gradually began visiting the poor and ill in their families and others all crowded together in the surrounding squalid shacks, inquiring about their needs.

Teresa found a never-ending stream of human needs in the poor she met, and frequently was exhausted. Despite the weariness of her days she never omitted her prayer, finding it the source of support, strength and blessing for all her ministry.

A Movement Begins

Teresa was not alone for long. Within a year, she found more help than she anticipated. Many seemed to have been waiting for her example to open their own floodgates of charity and compassion. Young women came to volunteer their services and later became the core of her Missionaries of Charity. Others offered food, clothing, the use of buildings, medical supplies andMONEY.

Mother Teresa in Calcutta 109

As support and assistance mushroomed, more and more services became possible to huge numbers of suffering people.

From their birth in Calcutta, nourished by the faith, compassion and commitment of Mother Teresa, the Missionaries of Charity have grown like the mustard seed of the Scriptures. New vocations continue to come from all parts of the world, serving those in great need wherever they are found. Homes for the dying, refuges for the care and teaching of orphans and abandoned children, treatment centers and hospitals for those suffering from leprosy, centers and refuges for alcoholics, the aged and street people — the list is endless.

Until her death in 1997, Mother Teresa continued her work among the poorest of the poor, depending on God for all of her needs. Honors too numerous to mention had come her way throughout the years, as the world stood astounded by her care for those usually deemed of little value. In her own eyes she was "God's pencil — a tiny bit of pencil with which he writes what he likes."

Despite years of strenuous physical, emotional and spiritual work, Mother Teresa seemed unstoppable. Though frail and bent, with numerous ailments, she always returned to her work, to those who received her compassionate care for more than 50 years. Only months before her death, when she became too weak to manage the administrative work, she relinquished the position of head of her Missionaries of Charity. She knew the work would go on.

Finally, on September 5, 1997, after finishing her dinner and prayers, her weakened heart gave her back to the God who was the very center of her life.

THE CELEBRITY WITH NO PRIVATE LIFE

What is interesting about some of the opponents of Mother Teresa is that they are inclined to discredit her not directly, but by discrediting those who supported her. This is particularly the case with adversaries like Christopher Hitchens and Aroup Chatterjee. They dig deep into the private lives of anyone who

110 *Mother Teresa*

helped the nun to become an international celebrity. The numerous derogatory comments that Hitchens and Chatterjee make in their books against Malcolm Muggeridge, Robert S. McNamara, Dominique Lapierre or Ronald Reagan are at times rather too personal and insulting.

While both critics have raised some serious issues about the motives and nature of Mother Teresa's work in and outside India, their uncompromisingly hostile attitude towards her and those who supported her has undermined considerably the value of their criticism.

Likewise, some Indian opponents of the 'Saint of the Gutters', as the Indian press often refers to Mother Teresa, have ended up producing, either on purpose or unwittingly, what one could consider 'muck-raking' criticism.

The personal attacks mounted on Mother Teresa's supporters are partly related to their allegedly chequered pasts as well as their not-so-holy intentions in financing, endorsing and promoting the work of this particular Christian missionary.

One could interpret such attacks as an indication of the pent-up frustration and failure of Mother Teresa's committed opponents to uncover something embarrassing and humiliating about the nun herself. The unprecedented media attention Mother Teresa generated for almost fifty years in India and throughout the world was bound to expose many personal details about her. Being a celebrity, it was inevitable that her life would become 'public property', that people would want to know as much as possible about the woman behind the nun.

The vast literature on this religious celebrity, however, would disappoint anyone hoping to find there revealing details about the private Mother Teresa. Accounts of her personal life remain rather sketchy even in the best authorized and unauthorized biographies. Both her subjectivist admirers and her structuralist opponents have failed to produce a complete biography of Agnes Gonxhe Bojaxhiu. As for those who approach her figure from a post-structuralist position, they too have been unable so far to 'uncover' the woman behind the missionary.

Mother Teresa in Calcutta

While Mother Teresa was undoubtedly a 'media star', analysing her life along the straightforward post-structuralist lines employed when commenting on the lives of stars from the fields of the media, sport, music and cinema remains problematic.

The star discourse emerged for the first time in the United States in the early 1910s when interest in actors went beyond their screen roles.

John Belton holds that:

[a]ctors develop a persona or portrait of themselves out of the personalities of the various characters they have played over the course of their careers and out of elements of their personal lives that have become public knowledge.

With the press becoming ever more inquisitive and intrusive, many famous actors found it impossible to keep details of their personal lives out of the public gaze. Media played a crucial role in the transformation of actors into stars.

As Christine Gledhill notes, '[a]ctors become stars when their off-screen life-styles and personalities equal or surpass acting ability in importance'.

As a result of the information about the actors' personal lives made public by the media, the attention of many film fans shifted from the screen characters to the real people who portrayed them. This important shift was possible because of the emergence of what Richard deCardova calls the 'star scandal' discourse. The unprecedented interest the public started showing in the stars' inti-mate lives transformed not only the relationship between actors and their admirers, but also redefined the notion of fame for screen actors.

The 'star scandal' thus became an irreplaceable stepping stone to fame (or infamy) and celebrity status not only in twentieth-century America and other developed countries but also across the developing world.

While the 'star scandal' obviously plays a crucial role in the lives and careers of stars from the world of entertainment, politics and sport, it hardly had any significant impact on the celebrity status of Mother Teresa.

112   *Mother Teresa*

This does not mean that she was and remains immune from controver-sial stories. On the contrary, thanks to the relentless efforts of opponents like Hitchens and Chatterjee to reveal the 'real' Mother Teresa, the contro-versial has always been an important part in the often heated debates about her.

Claims that Mother Teresa accepted preferential treatment in India and overseas, that she travelled in luxury, that she was treated in expensive clinics and mishandled millions of dollars are a familiar theme in the ever-growing critical literature about her.

In spite of such sustained iconoclastic attacks on her figure, during her lifetime and after her death her image has hardly been dented seriously. So far her avowed opponents appear to have been unable to produce the 'killer' evidence that would irreparably damage Mother Teresa's reputation.

The main reason why Mother Teresa has apparently remained immune for so long from the 'star scandal' is because, unlike most stars, she does not seem to have suffered from the tensions resulting from the dichotomy between the *public face* a celebrity has to promote all the time, and the *private self*, or what Chris Rojek calls, the 'veridical self', which the star tries to protect fanatically but often without success.

In Mother Teresa's case, the private and the personal appear to have been one and the same thing. Although, like any other international 'star', she was constantly under media 'surveillance', throughout her long public life Mother Teresa never had to lash out at any photographer as the actor Johnny Depp did in London in 1999: 'I don't want to be what you want me to be tonight.' It appears that Mother Teresa was unique among twentieth-century celebrities in that she could be in public what she was in private. This was quite an achievement for Mother Teresa and for those who supported and promoted her in a world that teems with paparazzi who are always scandal-hunting and thus undermining the careers of all sorts of famous people, including religious celebrities.

As a seasoned public figure Mother Teresa apparently succeeded where many media stars usually fail. Not only did she

Mother Teresa in Calcutt a   **113**

seem able to establish very good contacts with journalists, but she also appeared to have cast a spell on them.

For her devoted supporters, the reporters' veneration for Mother Teresa was, and remains, yet another proof of her 'saintliness'. Bob Geldof, however, found 'nothing other-worldly or divine about her' when he met her in 1985. If Bob found anything extraordinary about his 'saintly' fellow charity worker, it was her skilful handling of the media.

She struck him as 'outrageously brilliant' in the way she handled reporters: 'She made them laugh and she defined the terms of the questions they could ask her.'

'The way she spoke to the journalists,' concluded Geldof, 'showed her to be as deft a manipulator of media as any high-powered American PR expert.'To a large extent, Mother Teresa's good relations with the media and her ability as a 'deft manipulator' were made possible and tolerated mainly because of the high moral ground she occupied as a result of her charity work and simple preaching for almost seventy years in India and throughout the world.

Mother Teresa was very much aware of this 'moral ground' which, to quote Geldof, 'gave her the right to march up to airlines and ask for a free ticket to Washington, and once she arrived, to ask to see the President of the United States knowing he dare not refuse her'.

No political, religious and business support would have kept Mother Teresa in the public eye for five successive decades unless the propaganda machine and the news industry had paid exclusive attention to her humanitarian work.

The nun's status as an exemplary media icon is likely to remain secured for as long as the media focus exclusively on her self-lessness and devotion to 'human debris'.

It is mainly thanks to the media that the celebrity Mother Teresa has entered the consciousness of our age as the epitome of compassion for humanity. Whether she deserves this status or not is something that will continue to divide her admirers and supporters in the years to come. What is certain, however, is that

114   *Mother Teresa*

in our sceptical age nobody's sanctity can be taken for granted for too long, not even the sanctity of a media untouchable like Mother Teresa.

The history of mankind is the history of its great men: the important thing is to find these out... clean the dirt from them... and place them on their proper pedestals. Thomas Carlyle *Patriotism is when love of your own people comes first; nationalism, when hate for people other than your own comes first.*

Charles de Gaulle

Lying is a form of our [Serbian] patriotism and is evidence of our innate intelligence. We live in a creative, imaginative and inventive way. In these lands every lie becomes a truth in the end.

The Macedonian Slavs and Mother Teresa

The controversies between the Macedonian Slavs and the Albanians over the origin of Alexander the Great, Skanderbeg and Mother Teresa could be interpreted as signs of an identity crisis which the new state of Macedonia is going through in the wake of its independence in the early 1990s.

While it has been widely acknowledged that the Illyrians were the ancient predecessors of the Albanians, the present-day Macedonians' claim that they are the descendants of the ancient Macedonians remains wishful thinking. The Slavs started settling in the Balkans from the third to the seventh century AD. Ancient Macedonia itself was colonized by the Slavs in the seventh century AD.

Ethnically, culturally and, more importantly, linguistically speaking the Macedonian Slavs have little connection with the ancient Macedonian ethnicity, culture and language. Ancient Macedonia had its beginnings in the eighth century BC, began to flourish in the fifth century BC, reached its zenith during the reigns of Philip II and Alexander, and ceased to have any significance as an ancient power after 146 BC when it became a Roman province.

Following the collapse of Rome, Macedonian territories came under the authority of the Byzantines, Bulgarians, Greeks, Albanians, Turks and Serbs. Present-day Macedonia emerged as an independent state in 1991 following its secession from the former Yugoslavia. The christening of this new country 'Macedonia' did not go down very well in the Balkans.

Bulgaria and Greece, for instance, have traditionally seen Macedonia as part of 'their' territories, which explains why these two countries, especially Greece, took issue not only with the name of 'Macedonia' but also with its very existence as an

116   *Mother Teresa*

independent state. This is a dispute which, if it gets out of control, could easily destabilize an already tense Balkans.

While the new Macedonia that emerged after the collapse of Yugoslavia is officially a multi-ethnic state, it is the Macedonian Slavs who still have the final say on how the country is run. In an effort to present themselves as a nation that can be taken seriously in the region and beyond, the Macedonian Slavs pay too much attention to the 'Macedonian identity', which essentially means Macedonian Slav identity. This policy has hardly endeared non-Slavic communities to the Macedonian Slavs, especially the Albanians who, according to figures released in December 2003 by the Macedonian Institute for Statistics, make up 25.17 per cent of the country's population.

The discriminatory practices apparent in governmental departments, police force and education were some of the causes of the armed conflict in spring 2001 between the Macedonian state and Albanian guerrilla fighters, who demanded equal rights for the Albanian population. The prompt intervention of the international community fortunately avoided the escalation of the conflict, but this country may face further difficulties.

The raging war of words on the ethnicity of Mother Teresa and Skanderbeg indicates that the two major ethnic groups in the Republic of Macedonia are becoming increasingly sensitive about and over-protective of their cultural heritage, history and heroes.

The row over Mother Teresa's origin is particularly interesting in view of the fact that, unlike Alexander the Great and Skanderbeg, she did not live in the distant past. One would normally assume that in Mother Teresa's case there should be no room for biographical ambiguities because everything about her life and work can be easily traced and verified. Many people who knew her intimately as a child, as a young girl and as a nun are still alive and they can clarify any detail about her life and work that has been reported inaccurately either by mistake or on purpose.

Determining Mother Teresa's ethnic origin should not be difficult also because, unlike her two illustrious Balkan expatriates, Alexander the Great and Skanderbeg, she was not royalty. Nor did she come from an ancient aristocratic family that had to use

The Macedonian Slavs and Mother Teresa 117

inter-ethnic marriages to consolidate, maintain or expand its power and influence.

This does not mean, however, that Mother Teresa was a 'commoner', or a Balkan 'peasant', as most of her Western and Indian friends and opponents maintain indirectly or openly in their books. Both parents of the 'plebeian' nun came from well-to-do families that had earned their fortune through hard work over several generations.

It is true that her parents' marriage was an arranged one, and that their families' wealth and social status played a role in bringing them together. Both parents, however, were born in Albania and were Albanians. Mother Teresa's brother Lazar Bojaxhiu emphasized all the time that his parents and their descendants were Albanians from Kosova, his mother's family being originally from Novosela near the town of Gjakova, and that of his father from Prizren.

For reasons which will be explained later in this chapter and in chapter four, Mother Teresa herself was never keen to mention her nationality when she talked to the press. There were occasions, however, when she made it absolutely clear that she was Albanian. So, for example, when she was awarded the Nobel Peace prize in Oslo in 1979 she told the curious international media during one of the ceremonies that '[b]y blood and origin I am *all Albanian*' (emphasis added). Considering that Mother Teresa's brother and, more importantly, Mother Teresa herself were always consistent about their Albanian origin, it makes no sense to argue that her descent is far from clear. Surely Mother Teresa was the best authority on the issue of her ethnic origin.

The Macedonian Slavs have always been aware of the fact that, as far as her ethnicity is concerned, Mother Teresa never pretended that she was anything other than Albanian. All the same, this has not stopped some of them casting doubt on her Albanian roots. Macedonia has its fair share of Mother Teresa experts among the Macedonian Slavs and the Albanians who have recently tried hard to find in a few hand-picked letters, speeches and remarks of Mother Teresa crumbs of evidence of her 'lifetime' attachment and devotion either to Macedonia or Albania.

118

Mother Teresa

Some Macedonian Slav artists, scholars, reporters and politicians, who have taken a keen interest in and have written widely on her, such as Tome Serafimovski, Jasmina Mironski and Stojan Trenãevski, the president of the association 'Skopje Woman Mother Teresa', are keen to score points over their Albanian rivals not only with regard to the fact that, in their view, she spoke little or no Albanian but, more importantly, that during one of her visits to Skopje she refused to give a straightforward answer when asked repeatedly if she was Albanian, Macedonian, Vlach, Serbian or of any other nationality. 'I am a citizen of Skopje, the city of my birth,' she told the reporters eventually, 'but I belong to the world.' During the same visit, referring to the 1963 earthquake, whichh adal mostf lattenedh ern ativec ity,s her emarked:' Itm ay look completely different, but it is still my Skopje.'

For a devoted Roman Catholic like Mother Teresa, 'my Skopje' did not necessarily mean the capital of the predominantly Orthodox Christian Republic of Macedonia. Nor did she refer to the city of her birth as 'my Skopje' purely because it had been inhabited by Albanians since ancient times. The possessive adjective 'my' in this case refers to the Skopje of her childhood memories, something she was keen to emphasize repeatedly: 2

If there were not so much concrete we could be walking on the pavements of the streets where I spent *my childhood*. I am glad to see these places again. At least for a short time I am back in *my childhood*. (emphasis added)

More importantly, perhaps, Mother Teresa referred to the city of her birth as 'my Skopje' because of its sixteen centuries of documented Catholic legacy. Ancient Skopje was one of the region's thriving cities during Roman and Byzantine times. The Illyrians, like the Greeks, came into contact with Christianity during the Apostolic age. In 'The Letter of Paul to the Romans', the apostle states that 'from Jerusalem and as far around as Illyricum I have fully proclaimed the good news of Christ'. The ancestors of the present-day Albanians were among the first Europeans to convert to Christianity. As early as the first century AD, they had established in the city of Dyrrachium (present-day Durrës) one of the world's earliest bishoprics. By the end of the third century AD, the

The Macedonian Slavs and Mother Teresa 119

Albanians were Christianized. This means that they became Christians over a century before the pagan Roman conquerors underwent their 'conversion of convenience', and at least six centuries before any of the neighbouring Slav nations, including the Macedonian Slavs, decided to adopt Europe's 'official' religion.

Mother Teresa's Skopje had its own bishop by the fourth century AD, and since then some of the Albanians in the town have remained faithful to the teachings of Christ. Skopje's loyalty to Christianity, obviously, made the city of her birth very special to the devoted Albanian Catholic nun because it symbolized her own people's exemplary attachment to Christ. It was primarily in this respect, one could argue, that Skopje had a special place in her heart, and why she, it is claimed, called herself a 'Skopjanka', someone from Skopje.

For some Macedonian Slavs, however, an Albanian Mother Teresa apparently was and still remains unacceptable for several reasons. Like the Serbs, the Macedonian Slavs have considered the Albanians a millen-nium-old obstacle to the colonization of some parts of the Balkans. Throughout their long struggle for national survival, though, the Albanians have never considered the Macedonian Slavs a serious threat. Their greatest danger has always come from the Serbs whose dream of colonizing the Albanian territories started as early as the ninth century. The following discussion on Serbia's territorial ambitions over lands populated by the Albanians may seem like an unnecessary digression from the topic in ques-tion and from the main focus of the book but is vital to an understanding of the reasons why the Macedonian Slavs, like the Serbs, are far from happy to admit that Mother Teresa was Albanian, and are determined to 'prove' the Albanians wrong.

Finding a 'final solution' to the Albanian 'obstacle' that has always undermined Serbia's overt ambition for absolute control over the southern Balkans has consistently been at the heart of the Serbian expansionist policy. This is articulated very clearly in 'The Expulsion of the Albanians' memorandum. This revealing document, which represents the 'bible' of the uncompromising Serbian colonialist policy, was penned by Vaso âubriloviç, a Serbian

120   *Mother Teresa*

academic and statesman who was a member of the group that plotted the assassination of Archduke Franz Ferdinand in 1914. The memorandum was presented to the government of Milan Stoyadinovic (1935-1939) in Belgrade on 7 March 1937.

Incidentally, this Serbian-born prime minister and academic was one of several Serbian politicians and intellectuals who ardently admired and supported both Hitler and Mussolini. After criticizing in his memorandum what he calls 'the slow and cumbersome strategy of gradual colonization' his country had followed in the past, âubriloviç puts forward a detailed strategy according to which Serbia would eventually get rid once and for all of the Albanians by deporting them *en masse* to Turkey and expelling the rest of them to Albania proper. He is confident that only 'the brute force of an organized state' and 'coercion by the state apparatus' would 'make staying intolerable for the Albanians' in their ancient homeland in Kosova.

The ethnically cleansed Albanian lands, he goes on, would then be populated with 'arrogant, ireascible and merciless' Montenegrins, who would eventually develop 'a less local and more broad-minded, Serbian out-look', and Serbian 'colonists' from impoverished parts of Serbia. Only by completely eradicating the Albanian population in Kosova, would Serbia finally consolidate its absolute control over 'this strategic point', which, to a large degree, determines 'the fate of the central Balkans'. Equally important for the Serbs, notes âubriloviç, is fulfilling the ambition to establish territorial contact with the Macedonian Slavs:

From an ethnic point of view, the Macedonians will only unite with us, if they receive true ethnic support from their Serbian motherland, something which they have lacked to this day. This can only be achieved through the destruction of the Albanian wedge.

1937 memorandum was followed by other similar and at times more vicious plans proposing even the complete elimination of the Albanian state, an idea first put forward in the London Treaty of 26 April 1915. Such plans were formulated during World War II by several Serbian intellectuals and politicians including Ivan Vukotiç, Stevan Moljeviç, and the 1961 Nobel Prize laureate

The Macedonian Slavs and Mother T eresa   121

for literature Ivo Andriç. âubriloviç himself submitted a second memorandum on 3 November 1944, this time entitled 'The Minority Problem in the New Yugoslavia', arguing that '[t]he democratic federation of Yugoslavia will only achieve peace and ensure its development if it can be made ethnically pure'. As in the first memorandum, âubriloviç is adamant that the only way to do this is to follow the example of the Third Reich in dealing with the 'alien element'.

According to âubriloviç, all minorities in Yugoslavia 'deserve to lose their right of citizenship'. âubriloviç believes that the expulsion of ethnic minorities, especially of the Albanians in Kosova, would be carried out efficiently only by the military. In his words, 'the army must be brought in, even during the war, to cleanse the regions we wish to settle with our own people, doing so in a well-planned but ruthless manner'. By now âubriloviç is careful not to give the impression to fellow Slavic nations, especially Croatia, that he has only the interests of Serbia at heart.

Although this demagogue is eager to sound more like a 'Yugoslav' citizen than someone masterminding Serbian expansionist policy, he makes no secret of his ultimate goal, which is Serbia's ethnic conquest of Kosova. Only by completely colonizing all the Albanian lands in the south of the Balkans on behalf of Serbia, âubriloviç concludes, '[are we] to reach our goal of linking Montenegro, Serbia and Macedonia'.

Like most other Slavs living in the republics comprising the former Yugoslavia, the Macedonian Slavs were also unhappy with the influence the Serbs wanted to exert in the running of the federation that emerged after the Second World War. Unlike other fellow Slavs, however, the Macedonian Slavs were more inclined to put up with 'the jailer of the other Yugoslav nations', as Serbia was often referred to within the federation and internationally, because of the Serbs' uncompromising stance on the issue of the complete colonization of the Albanian lands south of their border.

As far as the Macedonian Slavs are concerned, a Kosova without Albanians would weaken significantly the Albanian community in the Republic of Macedonia. The Macedonians Slavs have never been able to implement any plan to ethnically cleanse

122   *Mother Teresa*

the Albanians living in Albanian lands in the Republic of Macedonia on the scale and with the openness pursued for so long by the Serbs. On the other hand, like the Serbs, they have always been eager to denigrate the Albanians and anything Albanian. The official, degrading discourse employed by numerous Serbian leaders, epitomized in the racist remarks of the Serbian prime minister Vladan Djordjeviç (1844–1930), who saw the Albanians as 'pre-humans',is also present in the rhetoric of some Macedonian Slav and Montenegrin politicians and intellectuals, the main aim of which is to deny Albanians their Illyrian descent and present them as 'uncivilized'.

By demonizing the Albanians relentlessly, the Serbian-led Slavic coali-tion hoped that the Western powers would in the end allow them to eliminate completely this non-Slavic nation. After all, by getting rid of the Albanian 'savages', the Serbs and their fellow Montenegrin and Macedonian Slavs were apparently doing a huge favour to Western Europe. It was imperative that the West should perceive these three allies' coloniza-tion of the Albanian lands as 'absolutely necessary' to avoid an 'imminent danger' awaiting Europe by the 'non-European' Albanians.

To achieve this ambitious task, the Serbian politicians needed some-thing of an ideological footing. The Serbian army and its Slavic mercenaries could not do the job properly unless their brutality was backed up with 'scholarly' and 'scientific' arguments that 'justified' the disintegration, assimilation and finally the elimination of the Albanian nation as a must to safeguard not so much Serbia's interests but the very future of Western civilization.

Vaso âubriloviç believed that 'the expulsion of the Albanians as quickly as possible and resettlement by our colonists' required 'close collaboration between the government, private initiative and scholarly institutions'. He was adamant that Serbian intellectuals in particular had a vital role to play in 'selling' Serbia's colonial policy to the Serbian people and, more importantly, to Western Europe as perfectly 'rational'. In a tone which is both admonishing and inviting, in his 1937 mem-orandum âubriloviç drew attention to the fact that Serbian educational and research institutions have begun to lose the prestige they once had.... Many

The Macedonian Slavs and Mother T eresa

billions would have been saved in this country, many mistakes would have been avoided in our government policy, including our colonization policy, had the problems been studied seriously and objectively in advance by competent scholars before they were taken up for solution.

Our policy of colonization, likewise, would have acquired a more serious approach, greater continuity and effective application, had the opinions of experts and scholars been sought in advance. To start with, the Royal Serbian Academy of Sciences and the University of Belgrade ought to take the initiative to organize *scientific studies of the whole problem of colonization* in our country. This would be feasible for many reasons. At the university we have experts on every aspect of colonization. Teachers and academicians at the university are independent scholars, less subject to external political influence. They already have good experience in such fields and their scholarly work is a guarantee of objectivity. They should, therefore, take the initiative of setting up a *colonization institute*, the task of which would be to pursue *colonization studies*. (emphasis added)

As is obvious from âubriloviç's assessment, Serbian academics have always been loyal adherents and nurturers of the Serbian dream of domination of the Balkans. In âubriloviç's own words, his scholarly fellow countrymen 'already have good experience in such fields'. Being a university professor himself, âubriloviç was, of course, speaking as a well-informed insider. What âubriloviç was asking of his colleagues now was that they be much more active and sophisticated during the renewed and well-funded campaign to present all non-Serbs living in territories ruled by Belgrade, especially the Albanians in Kosova and across Yugoslavia, as racially inferior, cultureless and historyless.

The constant onslaught on Albanian history, language, culture and tradition waged by numerous Serbian, Montenegrin and Macedonian Slav scholars, the attempt to present the Albanians as a nation with no heroes of their own, and the claim that most noted Albanian national leaders, poets, artists, linguists and scientists are not of Albanian origin, were meant to further humiliate this ancient and proud nation. This carefully orchestrated

124   *Mother Teresa*

propaganda campaign to besmear the Albanians has been constantly challenged but never more seriously than in the case of Mother Teresa. Her emergence as an international humanitarian icon inevitably shattered as never before the Serbian myth that the Albanians were 'barbarians'. How could someone like Mother Teresa, who came to epitomize the best of human spirit in a century dominated by savage wars and bloodshed, come from 'Albanian stock'?

Surely, a nation of 'thieves', 'hooligans', 'thugs', 'arsonists', 'kidnappers', 'drug-dealers', 'rapists', 'human traffickers', 'terrorists' and 'pimps' (some of the derogatory terms used by Serbian and Macedonian propaganda to demonize the Albanians) who have always caused 'problems' among the Slavs in the Balkans, 'initiated' the disintegration of Yugoslavia, and are currently posing a grave danger to Western civilization with their 'obvious' links to the international mafia, could not produce a dove of peace like Mother Teresa. It was only logical, therefore, that Mother Teresa was not, could not, and should not be Albanian. If she could not be a Macedonian Slav, a Serb or a Croat, she must certainly be a Vlach, a Roma, a Venetian –anything but an Albanian.

Mother Teresa was and appears still to be unacceptable to the Serbs and the Macedonian Slavs not only for her humanitarian spirit but, more importantly, also for her staunch faith. The Serbs' vitriolic attacks on Albanian culture, history, language, tradition and personalities, attacks which, as Cubriloviç admits with disturbing frankness, after 1878 included 'secretly razing Albanian villages and urban settlements to the ground' with 'great practical effect', have somehow served their purpose to alienate some European countries from the Albanians. Such acts of vandalism, however, were never deemed effective enough to completely demonize the Albanians in the eyes of all the European nations. For the Albanians to be seen as a constant 'grave peril' to Europe, they had to be presented as a 'mob' that 'endangered' the very 'essence' of modern European 'identity': Christianity.

Many Serbian scholars in conjunction with the Serbian Orthodox Church believed that they had finally found in Islam the most efficient weapon with which to humiliate the unruly

The Macedonian Slavs and Mother T eresa 125

Albanians and alienate them forever from Europe. The plan was simple but had far-reaching conse-quences. The Serbs were to present themselves as a nation with a biblical mission in the second millennium, a mission which included stopping the advance of the Ottomans and, more importantly, crushing a 'demonic' people like the Albanians, who were 'dangerous' to Europe not only because they were 'uncivilized', but also because they were not Christians, and, even worse, because some of them had committed the dreadful sin of apostasy. Obviously, the Serbs were indispensable if Christianity were to remain Europe's uncontested religion.

The myth of the Serbs as defenders and martyrs of the Christian faith has its roots in the misrepresentation of an important event in the history of the Balkans, the Battle of Kosova. This infamous battle is in essence a remarkable show of unity on the part of several Balkan rulers deter-mined to oppose the advance of the Ottomans in the Balkans. The Balkan rebels must have caused the Turkish Sultan quite a headache to have made him order and lead himself a fearsome punitive expedition against them. The major battle between Murat I's army and the Balkan alliance troops took place on the Plain of Kosova in June 1389. In spite of their unity and valour, the Balkan coalition proved to be no match for the mighty Ottoman army.

The Balkan resistance this time was led by Prince Lazar of Serbia, but the alliance itself included many nationalities from the region, including the Albanians. For several centuries to come, this fourteenth-century battle was a bitter memory for many Balkan nations, a painful reminder of a common defeat against a common enemy.

In the nineteenth century, however, Serbian nationalists and the Serbian Orthodox Church, helped by some collectors of Serbian epics and poets such as Vuk Karadziç and Petar II Petroviç-Njegos, claimed that the battle was a key event only in the history of the Serbian nation. This meant that the 1389 defeat ceased to be a Balkan defeat; instead it became exclusively a Serbian defeat. This battle, the Serbs have claimed for more than a hundred years, is testimony to the Serbian nation's suffering in the name of Christ.

The conversion of some Albanian rulers to Islam in the wake of the 1433–1468 Skanderbeg-led Albanian resistance was used by some nineteenth-century Serbian politicians, scholars and leaders of the Serbian Orthodox Church to present the Albanians as non-Christian, and as such a non-indigenous European people. According to the new Serbian version of the Battle of Kosova, the Albanians had not fought alongside the Serbs against the Turks but on the side of the Turks against Prince Lazar's army. Serbian propaganda was eager to paint all Albanian Muslims as Turks or Islamicized Serbs, and every Albanian national movement as an Albanian attempt to establish a Muslim state at the heart of Christian Europe. The Serbs employed the rhetoric of the crusaders to give legitimacy to their colonization policy across Albanian lands.

That the Serbs waged terror against the Albanians not simply because they allegedly wanted to defend Christianity but primarily because they intended to colonize their lands is obvious from the brutality they showed at the start of the twentieth century against both Muslim and Catholic Albanians. Attempts were made to coerce Albanian Catholics to renounce Catholicism and convert forcibly to the Orthodox faith. Faced with conversion or death, some Albanian Catholics apostasized; those who refused were massacred.

As in similar earlier campaigns, the Serbs appropriated Albanian churches and other religious sites, thus reinforcing the myth that Kosova was the cradle not just of the Serbian nation but more importantly of their proverbial devotion to Christianity. The Orthodox Serbs' employment of 'religious rhetoric to justify the defence of "sacred" Serbian interests,' holds Noel Malcolm, is 'a classic example of religion being mobilized and manipulated for ideological purposes'. This mobilization and manipulation of religion was apparent throughout the existence of Yugoslavia. Some Albanians in the Yugoslav federation were rather naïve at times in seeing Islam as 'their' national religion, but they were also conveniently 'helped' by the Yugoslav authorities, especially the Serbs, and the Macedonian Slavs to distance themselves from Christianity and stick to 'their' Islamic 'roots'.

The Macedonian Slavs and Mother Teresa

So, for instance, while on the one hand the Albanians in the post World War II Yugoslavia were constantly prohibited from baptizing their children with Albanian names, on the other hand, they were always encouraged to use Muslim names instead.

Likewise, throughout the twentieth century, while Serbian and Macedonian governments constantly forbade the Albanians from opening schools in their native language, they would welcome any effort on the part of the Albanians to build mosques or open *madrasas*. In a Yugoslavia that followed an openly discriminating policy in employment towards the Albanians, becoming an *imam* was one of the few career opportunities open to many young Albanians.

According to Sokol Shameti, this is the main reason behind the surplus of *imams* in Macedonia.

The 'traditional good will' of the Yugoslav, Serbian and Macedonian authorities towards the Albanians' 'religious sentiments' explains why in Albania proper, in contrast to Kosova and Macedonia, Islam is not, and never has been, seen as an integral part of Albanian national identity, but mainly as a legacy of the Ottoman occupation.

The Serbs mobilized and manipulated religion, especially throughout the 1990s when the Serbian ultranationalists led by Slobodan Miloseviç were largely responsible for the disintegration of Yugoslavia. In his 1984 address to the members of the League of Communists at the University of Belgrade, Miloseviç made it clear that he foresaw a leading role for the Serbian Orthodox Church in interpreting the interests of the Serbian nation.

As in the past, throughout the wars that engulfed Yugoslavia at the end of the twentieth century, it was the Serbian Orthodox Church that originated and sustained the discourse according to which the Serbs were the 'martyred Christians' of the Balkans whom Europe must listen to and help.

The Serbian Orthodox Church was instrumental in gener-ating the 'promised land' theme employed constantly by Miloseviç and his team of fanatic nationalists during the Kosova war of 1999 in an attempt to present their ethnic cleansing policy against the

128   *Mother Teresa*

Albanians as a God-given mission to defend not just their Christian heritage in Kosova but also the whole of Christendom from the Muslims.

As during the time of Cubriloviç, even when Yugoslavia was falling apart, fanatical Serbian nationalists and the Serbian Orthodox Church relied heavily on their traditional allies, Serbian academics. Several Serbian scholars and journalists-turned-politicians like Dobrica Cosiç, Vojislav Kostunica and Vuk Draskoviç remain staunch supporters of the now-discredited thesis regarding the legitimacy of the Serbs' claim over Kosova as the holy cradle of Serbia. Much to the Serbs' disappointment, the Europe of the 1990s had changed considerably from the Europe that at the beginning of the twen-tieth century had kept quiet about or, even worse, condoned the atrocities committed by the Serbian army against the Albanians.

The intervention of the international community to stop the ethnic cleansing of Kosova in 1999 indicated that the Western powers were no longer duped by, and some were unwilling to have anything to do with, Serbia's rhetoric and colonization policy in the southern Balkans, at least not publicly. Eighty-six years after the dismemberment of the Albanian nation at the London Conference in 1913, a dismemberment which came about partly as a result of Serbian propaganda about the 'danger' the Albanian Muslims appar-ently posed to Christian Europe, the West finally decided not to ignore any longer the Albanians' plight. Obviously, the Albanian question had never been an Islamic question in the first place.

Following the example of the extreme Serbian nationalists and of the Serbian Orthodox Church, many Macedonian Slav politicians, religious leaders, intellectuals and reporters were eager to present the Albanian guerrilla fighters during the 2001 conflict not as frustrated individuals who were fed up with being treated as second-class citizens in their own country and were determined to put an end to institutionalized discrimination and racism, but as Islamic terrorists. Human Rights Watch expressed concerns about 'endemic police abuse' against the Albanians in Macedonia in 1996, 1998 and again in 2001. Like the Serbs, the Macedonian

The Macedonian Slavs and Mother Teresa

Slavs failed in their attempts to convince the Western powers that 9the outraged Albanians in Macedonia were Muslim separatists. Partly because of the pressure from the international community and partly because it was obvious that they could not put down on their own the growing Albanian armed resistance, the government of Macedonia had no option but to sign the Ohri Peace Agreement in August 2001.

Even after the agreement, many Macedonian Slav intellectuals and politicians kept on 'warning' Europe of the Islamic 'danger' coming from the Albanians.

Unable to provide any valid proof of their accusations, they tried hard to establish a link between the Albanians in Kosova and Macedonia, the Albanian state and Al-Qaeda in the wake of the terrorist attacks against the United States of America on 11 September 2001.

Often during his trial at The Hague, where he was held accused of committing crimes against humanity, Slobodan Milo‰eviç tried, albeit without success, to 'enlighten' the UN tribunal regarding the notion that the Albanians and Osama Bin Laden are 'inseparable'. Milo‰eviç also claimed that his trial would fuel terrorism (read Islamic terrorism) in the Balkans. Articles of a sensationalist nature penned by several Western writers have been used unscrupulously in Serbian and Macedonian Slav propaganda as 'absolute proof' that the Albanians are 'guilty' as charged.

The news from the Vatican that Pope John Paul II was to beatify Mother Teresa in October 2003 obviously upset those Serbs and Macedonian Slavs who had been trying hard to vilify the Albanians, especially the guerrilla fighters in Kosova and in Tetova in Macedonia, as Muslim terrorists. As far as those who generated, used or hid behind the Serbian and Macedonian Slav propaganda were concerned, a Catholic nun like Mother Teresa, who was venerated as a 'saint' by millions of Christian and non-Christian believers and secular people worldwide when she was alive and who was well on the road to canonization only six years after her death, was not, could not and, more importantly, should not be Albanian.

Mother Teresa

Mother Teresa's Albanian origin, especially the fact that her parents came from an ancient Catholic Albanian family in the Albanian town of Prizren in Kosova, made a farce of the claim made by extremist Serbian nationalists and the Serbian Orthodox Church that the Albanians in Kosova were all Muslims.

Likewise, the fact that she was born to Albanian parents settling down and prospering amidst the ancient thriving Catholic Albanian community in Skopje meant that the ultranationalists among the Macedonian Slavs and some leaders of the Macedonian Orthodox Church, too, had to reconsider their long-held line about the Albanians in Macedonia being non-native or all Muslims.

That some Macedonian Slavs were and still are far from happy to admit that Mother Teresa was Albanian is apparent by the fact that in many conferences, symposiums, exhibitions, radio and television pro-grammes and documentaries, books and CD-ROMs dedicated to her in Macedonia, her Albanian roots are almost completely ignored.

In most cases, her ethnicity is mentioned mainly to emphasize that she was of a mixed-ethnic origin. To this day, Mother Teresa's name in the monuments dedicated to her in Skopje is written only in Cyrillic or English. Even her original Albanian name 'Gonxhe Bojaxhiu' is inscribed in English as 'Gondza Bojadziu'.

Only recently, as a result of the pressure exerted by Albanian politi-cians and intellectuals in Macedonia, and because their attempts to present Mother Teresa as a non-Albanian did not have any impact on the West's perception of her, some Macedonian Slav politicians have started making a few condescending remarks about Mother Teresa's Albanian origin. It is obvious that the Macedonian government can no longer afford to ignore the Catholic nun's Albanian roots.

For an impoverished country like Macedonia that is eager to join the European Union as soon as possible, Mother Teresa is seen as excellent PR, a means of showing Europe that freedom of religion and other civil and political rights are allegedly guaranteed by the Macedonian state equally to all ethnic groups in the country, including the Albanians. Mother Teresa, some Macedonian Slav politicians apparently believe, can help them to improve the

The Macedonian Slavs and Mother Teresa   131

country's recently tarnished image. And they may be right. The saint might not have seen herself as a Macedonian Slav, or a representative of the Republic of Macedonia when she trotted the globe as an international religious and media celebrity, but she can still be useful after her death to the former Yugoslav Republic of Macedonia, or the FYROM, as this country is still bizarrely known internationally. This is one of the reasons why in April 2006 the Macedonian parliament approved the 'Mother Teresa Award', which will be given to distinguished person-alities for their contribution to humanitarian work and culture.

MOTHER TERESA TAKES PRO-LIFE MESSAGE TO SUPREME COURT

Mother Teresa of Calcutta confronted President Clinton on his pro-abortion stand in early February at the National Prayer Breakfast. Last week she took her pro-life message to the highest court in the land. Her lawyers filed an amicus brief with the Supreme Court urging it to recognize the unborn child's inalienable right to life.

She urged the court to hear the case Alexander Loce vs. The State of New Jersey, which invol es the issue of whether or not the unborn child is a human being entitled to 14th Amendment protection. Loce was convicted of trespassing for attempting to prevent his fiance from having an abortion.

Mother Teresa's petition is a powerful witness in defense of life. It includes the following passage:

"America needs no words from me to see how your decision in Roe vs. Wade has deformed a great nation. The so-called right to abortion has pitted mothers against their children and women against men. It has sown violence and discord at the heart of the most intimate human relationships.

It has aggravated the derogation of the father's role in an increasingly fatherless society. It has portrayed the greatest of gifts — a child — as a competitor, an intrusion and an inconvenience. It has nominally accorded mothers unfettered dominion over the dependent lives of their physically dependent sons and daughters. And, in granting this unconscionable power, it has exposed many

132 *Mother Teresa*

women to unjust and selfish demands from their husbands or other sexual partners.

"Human rights are not a privilege conferred by government," she said. "They are every human being's entitlement by virtue of his humanity.

The right to life does not depend, and must not be contingent, on the pleasure of anyone else, not even a parent or sovereign. The Constitutional Court of the Federal Republic of Germany recently ruled: 'The unborn child is entitled to its right to life independently of its acceptance by its mother; this is an elementary and inalienable right which emanates from the dignity of the human being.'

"Americans may feel justly proud that Germany in 1993 was able to recognize the sanctity of human life. You must weep that your own government, at present, seems blind to this truth."

Prayers and Meditations

Into Paradise

May the Angels lead her into Paradise.

May the Martyrs receive her at her coming and take her to Jerusalem, the Holy City.

May the Choirs of the Angels receive her, and may she, with the once poor Lazarus, have rest everlasting. Amen. -The Roman Ritual

FOR A RELIGIOUS

All-powerful God,

out of love for Christ and his Church, Mother Teresa served you faithfully in the religious life.

May she rejoice at the coming of your glory

and enjoy eternal happiness

with her sisters in your kingdom.

We ask this through our Lord Jesus Christ, your Son,

who lives and reigns with you and the Holy Spirit,

one God for ever and ever.

The Macedonian Slavs and Mother Teresa **133**

FOR A WOMAN DECEASED

Lord, we beseech Thee, in the tenderness of Thy great mercy, to have pity upon the soul of Thy handmaid Mother Teresa, cleanse her from all defilements which have stained this mortal body, and give her inheritance in everlasting salvation. Through our Lord Jesus Christ, who with the Father and Holy Ghost liveth and reigneth world without end Amen.

Grant, O Lord, we beseech Thee, this mercy unto Thy servant deceased, that, having in desire kept Thy will, she may not suffer in requital of her deeds: and as a true Faith joined her unto the company of Thy faithful here below, so may Thy tender mercy give her place above, among the Angel choirs. Through Christ our Lord.

R. Amen.

V. Eternal rest grant unto her, O Lord.

R. And let perpetual light shine upon her.

V. May she rest in peace.

R. Amen.

V. May her soul, and the souls of all the faithful departed, through the mercy of God, rest in peace.

R. Amen.

To Thee, O Lord, do we commend the soul of Thy servant Mother Teresa, that being dead to the world she may live unto Thee; and whatsoever sins she has committed through the frailty of her mortal nature, do Thou, by the pardon of Thy most merciful love, wash away.

R. Amen.

O Almighty God, Judge of the living and the dead, so fit and prepare us, we beseech Thee, by Thy grace, for that last account which we must one day give; that, when the time of our appointed change shall come, we may look up to Thee with joy and comfort, and may at last be received, together with her whom Thou hast now taken from us, and with all that are near and dear to us, into that place of rest and peace where Thou shalt Thyself wipe away all tears from all eyes and where all our troubles and sorrows shall have an end, through the merits and for the sake of Jesus Christ, our Blessed Saviour and Redeemer. Amen

Prayer to the Heart of Jesus

Gentlest Heart of Jesus, ever present in the Blessed Sacrament, ever consumed with burning love for the poor captive souls in Purgatory, have mercy on the soul of Your departed servant.

Be not severe in Your judgment, but let some drops of Your Precious Blood fall upon her, and send, O merciful Saviour, Your angels to conduct her to a place of refreshment, light and peace. Amen.

For the Poor

Make us worthy, Lord, to serve those people throughout the world who live and die in poverty and hunger. Give them through our hands, this day, their daily bread, and by our understanding love, give them peace and joy. - *Mother Teresa of Calcutta*

For the Helpless Unborn

Heavenly Father, You created mankind in Your own image and You desire that not even the least among us should perish. In Your love for us, You entrusted Your only Son to the holy Virgin Mary. Now, in Your love, protect against the wickedness of the evil, those little ones to whom You have given the gift of life.

Prayer for a Deceased Person

O God, Whose property it is ever to have mercy and to spare, we beseech Thee on behalf of the soul of Thy servant whom Thou hast called out of this world; look upon her with pity and let her be conducted by the holy angels to paradise, her true country. Grant that she who believed in Thee and hoped in Thee may not be left to suffer the pains of the purgatorial fire, but may be admitted to eternal joys. Through Jesus Christ, Thy Son, our Lord, Who with Thee and the Holy Ghost liveth and reigneth world without end. Amen.

Pray an Our Father followed by a Hail Mary.

V. Eternal rest give unto her, O Lord;

R. And let perpetual light shine upon her.

All powerful God, we pray for our sister Mother Teresa, who responded to the call of Christ and pursued wholeheartedly the ways of perfect love.

Grant that she may rejoice on that day when your glory will be revealed and in company with all her brothers and sisters share for ever the happiness of your kingdom.

We ask this through Christ our Lord.

Reflections

James Cardinal Hickey

Homily – Mass for Mother Teresa

Basilica of the National Shrine of the Immaculate Conception

September 7, 1997

Archbishop Cacciavillan, Archbishop O'Brien

Msgr. Bransfield, brother priests & deacons, dear Sisters, Missionaries of Charity, dear friends in Christ:

136   *Mother Teresa*

All the world was saddened to learn of Mother Teresa's death last Friday. People from every continent, from every walk of life and from every persuasion grieved her loss and spoke of her with love. Again and again, she was praised as one of this century's great humanitarians.

That she was – but she was so much, much more. In truth, Mother Teresa's life and work cannot be explained apart from her clear, uncompromising Catholic faith and her profound love for the Lord Jesus. That is the key which unlocks who she was and what she did as a lover of the poor and a universally respected advocate for human life and dignity.

Indeed, a trustful faith expressed in loving deeds is the central theme of Mother Teresa's entire life. She lived what we just proclaimed in the Book of Wisdom: "Those who trust [in the Lord] shall understand truth and the faithful will abide with Him in love."

As a young woman growing up in her native Albania she experienced the faith of her parents. Successful and prosperous, they were also generous to those in need. From her father, a well-traveled merchant, the future Mother Teresa learned of human suffering in various parts of the world. From her parish priest, she learned about the foreign missions.

As she grew to adulthood, she sensed God's call to religious life and to missionary activity. At the age of 18 she accepted His call in faith and in loving trust by becoming a Sister of Loretto and by embarking to far-off India. It was in India that she received much of her religious formation deepening her already ardent faith and love. It was also in India that she encountered the poor as she labored in a hospital in Bengali, and later, in a school in Calcutta. Wherever she went and whatever she did, her faith and trust in Jesus prompted her to open her heart and hands to the poor.

Yet the Lord was asking more of her. He was asking her to dedicate her whole life to the poorest of the poor. In 1948, the Holy Father granted her permission to begin a new religious order, the Missionaries of Charity – dedicated to the poor and abandoned on the streets of Calcutta.

Prayer for a Deceased Person 137

All this she did as a woman of faith. Her philosophy of life was simple. She summed it up this way: "Give God permission" to work through you. "The work is God's work. The poor are the Lord's poor. Put yourself completely under the influence of Jesus, so that He may think His thoughts with your mind, [and] do His work through your hands."

The Jesus she knew in deep prayer she met also in the poor. At the very heart of her life and mission are the words from St. Matthew's Gospel: 'whatever you did for one of these least brothers, you did for me.' Truly, she recognized the Lord Jesus in the abandoned leper dying in the streets, in the person ravaged by AIDS, in the newborn baby in need of a home, in children, hungry and neglected – and she taught her sisters to do the same.

Mother told the story of two young sisters whom she sent out to help a dying person. Before they departed she reminded them how reverently the priest handles the Body of Christ at Mass. She told them to have the same reverence for the bodies of the poor and the dying. Three hours later the sisters returned and told Mother Teresa how they washed and cared for the dying man taken from the gutters. The youngest sister said to her: "Mother, for three hours we were touching the Body of Christ!"

Mother saw Jesus in the poor and the dying but she also led them to Jesus and His love. She did not pity the poor but loved and respected them as human beings called to eternal life and glory. Her goals were simple and straightforward: to comfort them in hunger and illness and to open their hearts to God's love. She knew they needed bread, but also the living word of God. She knew they needed water, but also peace, truth, and justice. She knew they needed a home but also a loving embrace and deep respect.

Mother's deep faith expressed in loving service eventually attracted the world's attention. She was sought after by the media and honored by world leaders. Never for a moment did she use the spotlight for herself. Rather, she mingled the world's spotlight with the light of Christ and then focused it on the human dignity of the poor and the humanity of the unborn child. In 1993, at a Congressional Prayer Breakfast, here in Washington, she challenged

138   *Mother Teresa*

our nation when she said: "Any country that accepts abortion is not teaching its people to love, but to use violence to get what they want." She wanted nothing from the world except respect for human life and the resources to serve the poor.

In these last days, some have asked if Mother Teresa's work will go forward after her death. In God's loving Providence, Mother Teresa's work will continue through her sisters, the Missionaries of Charity, under the loving guidance of Sister Nurmila, the Superior General. It will go forward through the intense prayer of the contemplative Missionaries of Charity and by the loving service rendered by Mother Teresa's sisters — in Calcutta, in Washington & throughout the world. God gave the Church and the world an extraordinary gift in Mother Teresa but He continues that gift in her sisters, and in the brothers, priests and lay workers associated with her mission.

Finally, dear friends, we commend Mother Teresa to the Lord with uttermost confidence. The Book of Revelation proclaims, "Happy are the dead who die in the Lord. They shall find rest from their labors for their good works accompany them." Even as we pray for the happy repose of Mother Teresa's soul, so also our eyes of faith can readily see her entering the Kingdom of God, there to meet Jesus face to face. But in heaven, as on earth, she will meet Jesus many times over — in the leper whom she picked up from the gutter, the AIDS patient who died a beautiful death, the homeless woman who found love in one of her convents. She will see Jesus in them again — Jesus glorified at the Father's right hand. And we pray that she will rejoice forever, accompanied by those whose lives she touched.

May the angels lead her to paradise.

May the martyrs welcome her.

May she rejoice in the Holy City Jerusalem

where Lazarus is poor no longer!

"Mother Teresa marked the history of our century with courage. She served all human beings by promoting their dignity and respect, and made those who had been defeated by life feel the tenderness of God." - Pope John Paul II

Prayer for a Deceased Person 139

"This is very difficult for me to talk about even by way of a written statement. The day I became a bishop I became very close to Mother Teresa. She visited with me many times in New York, in Rome and elsewhere. I celebrated Mass more frequently for her than I can remember. The world has lost a saint on earth, but gained an extraordinary powerful intercessor in heaven. I never knew anyone quite like Mother Teresa. I will find myself feeling a deep sense of personal loss for a long time. I am grateful for Mother Teresa's successor, Sister Nirmala, with whom I have established a close relationship. I know that she and all of the Missionary Sisters of Charity will continue to carry out the indescribable work that this one saintly woman has initiated. I do not have to pray 'may she rest in peace'; I am convinced that she is already in glory."

John Cardinal O'Connor, Archdiocese of New York

"It is a time of both sadness and joy for all our sisters. It is a time of sadness because we have lost a loved one who supported us in our desire to serve the Lord Jesus...We are joyful in the knowledge that Mother is with Our Heavenly Father." Sister Noreen, Superior at the Missionaries of Charity, Newark, NJ.

"The Catholic Church in our day, and especially in our corner of it here in Newark, has been enriched by the life of Mother Teresa. He stated that Mother Teresa was "a devoted religious daughter of the Church and an extraordinary missionary with tremendous zeal and energy. The witness of her life has been a model of simplicity, piety and charity." Archbishop Theodore McCarrick, Archdiocese of Newark

"The sisters indicated that they were comforted by the fact that Mother Teresa had died between the 'first Friday' feast of the Sacred Heart of Jesus and the 'first Saturday' feast of the Immaculate Heart of Mary." Michael Hurley, spokesman for the Archdiocese of Newark, NJ

"A heartfelt concern for the poor, the downtrodden and the rejected" during a special Mass yesterday. "She saw Jesus Christ in every single person," the cardinal said. "We must carry on her work." Anthony Cardinal Bevilacqua, Archdiocese of Philadelphia

140 *Mother Teresa*

"This evening, there is less love, less compassion, less light in the world. She leaves us a strong message, which has no borders and which goes beyond faith: helping, listening, solidarity."

French President Jacques Chirac

"She helped the poorest of the poor, gave them courage to live and the feeling of their worth, Mother Teresa will remain unforgotten and be an example after her death."

German Chancellor Helmut Kohl

"Just over two years ago, the Archdiocese of Atlanta, and all the citizens (of Atlanta) had the rare opportunity to enjoy a visit from Mother Teresa. Today, on the occasion of her passing into eternal life, we are moved to remember the impact of those few hours she spent with us then, and how her words still resound in our hearts today. Mother's good works will always be remembered — everyone must know and admit that — but more deeply still, we will remember the love that shone from within her heart — love that was fueled by absolute dedication to Jesus Christ, His Church, and His command that we should love one another. Not long ago, she expressed once more the simple fundamental axiom of Christian life: 'Let us keep the joy of loving in our hearts and share this joy with all we meet.' Mother Teresa certainly lived up to these words, and by her actions, taught their meaning to the whole world. She will long remain an inspiration to those who would serve the poor, and we bless God the Father for having shared the gift of Mother's life with us all."

Archbishop John F. Donoghue, Archdiocese of Atlanta

"She is the United Nations. She is peace in the world."

Former U.N. Secretary-General Javier Perez de Cuellar

"This beautiful Mother Teresa has opened for mankind the portals of heaven and shown us the Heart of God. Jesus is saying to her, 'Come, you blessed of My Father. I was hungry and you gave me to eat. I was thirsty and you gave me to drink. I was alone, forsaken, sick, abandon, poor, heartbroken, and desolate and you took me in. What you did to the least of these My Brethren, you did to me.' Mother Teresa had a Mother's heart, great and strong,

Prayer for a Deceased Person

and courageous enough to embrace the whole world. She will not soon be forgotten. Her reward will be great in Heaven. We pray for her and for those who follow her, that her work may go on. She has done something beautiful for God."

Sr. M. Raphael, PCPA, Our Lady Of Angels Monastary, Birmingham, Ala.

"The news of Mother Teresa's death is sad news: we shall miss her, with her warmth of spirit, her ability to talk about God and the prayer life which brings God so close to us. We shall miss her unique witness of care for the neediest of the needy for the love of God.

At the same time we give thanks to God for the wonderful memories Mother Teresa leaves us: her commitment to daily prayer, her building up of a worldwide network of religious sisters, brothers and priests who offer direct care to the suffering poor and homeless. In a special way we in Baltimore we are grateful to God for the ministry to those dying of AIDS carried out by the Missionaries of Charity in the Gift of Hope residence located here in St.

Wenceslaus Parish. Several years ago in Rome I had the privilege of working closely with her for the month-long meeting of the World Synod on the Consecrated Life, which brought together Catholic Church leaders, religious women and men, and delegates from other Christian churches to discuss at length the meaning of lives consecrated to God through vows.

Mother Teresa was assigned to the same English language discussion group as I, and all of us were impressed and touched by the depths of her convictions and the high spiritual quality of the insights which she shared with us. Mother Teresa leaves to all the world a legacy of faith and love and of concern for the poorest of the poor in the name of Jesus." Cardinal Keeler, Archdiocese of Baltimore

"The humanity of the world has lost its mother."

Congress Party President Sitaram Kesri

Prime Minister Inder Kumar Gujral called her "an apostle of peace and love."

142   *Mother Teresa*

"Mother Teresa never ceased to remind us that the greatest poverty of all is to live and to die unloved and unwanted. She demonstrated that love 'one person at a time'."

Roger Cardinal Mahony, Archdiocese of Los Angeles

Nobel Lecture

As we have gathered here together to thank God for the Nobel Peace Prize I think it will be beautiful that we pray the prayer of St. Francis of Assisi which always surprises me very much - we pray this prayer every day after Holy Communion, because it is very fitting for each one of us, and I always wonder that 4-500 years ago as St. Francis of Assisi composed this prayer that they had the same difficulties that we have today, as we compose this prayer that fits very nicely for us also. I think some of you already have got it - so we will pray together.

Let us thank God for the opportunity that we all have together today, for this gift of peace that reminds us that we have been created to live that peace, and Jesus became man to bring that good news to the poor. He being God became man in all things like us except sin, and he proclaimed very clearly that he had come to give the good news. The news was peace to all of good will and this is something that we all want - the peace of heart - and God loved the world so much that he gave his son - it was a giving - it is as much as if to say it hurt God to give, because he loved the world so much that he gave his son, and he gave him to Virgin Mary, and what did she do with him?

As soon as he came in her life - immediately she went in haste to give that good news, and as she came into the house of her cousin, the child - the unborn child - the child in the womb of Elizabeth, leapt with joy. He was that little unborn child, was the first messenger of peace. He recognised the Prince of Peace, he recognised that Christ has come to bring the good news for you and for me. And as if that was not enough - it was not enough to become a man - he died on the cross to show that greater love, and he died for you and for me and for that leper and for that man dying of hunger and that naked person lying in the street not only of Calcutta, but of Africa, and New York, and London, and

Prayer for a Deceased Person

Oslo - and insisted that we love one another as he loves each one of us. And we read that in the Gospel very clearly - love as I have loved you - as I love you - as the Father has loved me, I love you - and the harder the Father loved him, he gave him to us, and how much we love one another, we, too, must give each other until it hurts. It is not enough for us to say: I love God, but I do not love my neighbour.

St. John says you are a liar if you say you love God and you don't love your neighbour. How can you love God whom you do not see, if you do not love your neighbour whom you see, whom you touch, with whom you live. And so this is very important for us to realise that love, to be true, has to hurt. It hurt Jesus to love us, it hurt him. And to make sure we remember his great love he made himself the bread of life to satisfy our hunger for his love. Our hunger for God, because we have been created for that love. We have been created in his image. We have been created to love and be loved, and then he has become man to make it possible for us to love as he loved us. He makes himself the hungry one - the naked one - the homeless one - the sick one - the one in prison - the lonely one - the unwanted one - and he says: You did it to me. Hungry for our love, and this is the hunger of our poor people. This is the hunger that you and I must find, it may be in our own home.

I never forget an opportunity I had in visiting a home where they had all these old parents of sons and daughters who had just put them in an institution and forgotten maybe. And I went there, and I saw in that home they had everything, beautiful things, but everybody was looking towards the door. And I did not see a single one with their smile on their face. And I turned to the Sister and I asked: How is that?

How is it that the people they have everything here, why are they all looking towards the door, why are they not smiling? I am so used to see the smile on our people, even the dying one smile, and she said: This is nearly every day, they are expecting, they are hoping that a son or daughter will come to visit them. They are hurt because they are forgotten, and see - this is where love comes. That poverty comes right there in our own home, even

144 *Mother Teresa*

neglect to love. Maybe in our own family we have somebody who is feeling lonely, who is feeling sick, who is feeling worried, and these are difficult days for everybody. Are we there, are we there to receive them, is the mother there to receive the child?

I was surprised in the West to see so many young boys and girls given into drugs, and I tried to find out why - why is it like that, and the answer was: Because there is no one in the family to receive them.

Father and mother are so busy they have no time. Young parents are in some institution and the child takes back to the street and gets involved in something. We are talking of peace. These are things that break peace, but I feel the greatest destroyer of peace today is abortion, because it is a direct war, a direct killing - direct murder by the mother herself.

And we read in the Scripture, for God says very clearly: Even if a mother could forget her child - I will not forget you - I have carved you in the palm of my hand.

We are carved in the palm of His hand, so close to Him that unborn child has been carved in the hand of God. And that is what strikes me most, the beginning of that sentence, that even if a mother could forget something impossible - but even if she could forget - I will not forget you. And today the greatest means - the greatest destroyer of peace is abortion. And we who are standing here - our parents wanted us. We would not be here if our parents would do that to us.

Our children, we want them, we love them, but what of the millions. Many people are very, very concerned with the children in India, with the children in Africa where quite a number die, maybe of malnutrition, of hunger and so on, but millions are dying deliberately by the will of the mother. And this is what is the greatest destroyer of peace today. Because if a mother can kill her own child - what is left for me to kill you and you kill me - there is nothing between.

And this I appeal in India, I appeal everywhere: Let us bring the child back, and this year being the child's year: What have we done for the child? At the beginning of the year I told, I spoke

Prayer for a Deceased Person

everywhere and I said: Let us make this year that we make every single child born, and unborn, wanted. And today is the end of the year, have we really made the children wanted?

I will give you something terrifying. We are fighting abortion by adoption, we have saved thousands of lives, we have sent words to all the clinics, to the hospitals, police stations - please don't destroy the child, we will take the child.

So every hour of the day and night it is always somebody, we have quite a number of unwedded mothers - tell them come, we will take care of you, we will take the child from you, and we will get a home for the child.

And we have a tremendous demand from families who have no children, that is the blessing of God for us. And also, we are doing another thing which is very beautiful - we are teaching our beggars, our leprosy patients, our slum dwellers, our people of the street, natural family planning.

And in Calcutta alone in six years - it is all in Calcutta - we have had 61,273 babies less from the families who would have had, but because they practise this natural way of abstaining, of self-control, out of love for each other.

We teach them the temperature meter which is very beautiful, very simple, and our poor people understand. And you know what they have told me? Our family is healthy, our family is united, and we can have a baby whenever we want. So clear - those people in the street, those beggars - and I think that if our people can do like that how much more you and all the others who can know the ways and means without destroying the life that God has created in us.

The poor people are very great people. They can teach us so many beautiful things. The other day one of them came to thank and said: You people who have vowed chastity you are the best people to teach us family planning.

Because it is nothing more than self-control out of love for each other. And I think they said a beautiful sentence. And these are people who maybe have nothing to eat, maybe they have not a home where to live, but they are great people. The poor are very

146 *Mother Teresa*

wonderful people. One evening we went out and we picked up four people from the street. And one of them was in a most terrible condition - and I told the Sisters: You take care of the other three, I take of this one that looked worse. So I did for her all that my love can do. I put her in bed, and there was such a beautiful smile on her face. She took hold of my hand, as she said one word only: Thank you - and she died.

I could not help but examine my conscience before her, and I asked what would I say if I was in her place. And my answer was very simple. I would have tried to draw a little attention to myself, I would have said I am hungry, that I am dying, I am cold, I am in pain, or something, but she gave me much more - she gave me her grateful love. And she died with a smile on her face. As that man whom we picked up from the drain, half eaten with worms, and we brought him to the home. I have lived like an animal in the street, but I am going to die like an angel, loved and cared for.

And it was so wonderful to see the greatness of that man who could speak like that, who could die like that without blaming anybody, without cursing anybody, without comparing anything. Like an angel - this is the greatness of our people. And that is why we believe what Jesus had said: I was hungry - I was naked - I was homeless - I was unwanted, unloved, uncared for - and you did it to me.

I believe that we are not real social workers. We may be doing social work in the eyes of the people, but we are really contemplatives in the heart of the world. For we are touching the Body of Christ 24 hours. We have 24 hours in this presence, and so you and I.

You too try to bring that presence of God in your family, for the family that prays together stays together. And I think that we in our family don't need bombs and guns, to destroy to bring peace - just get together, love one another, bring that peace, that joy, that strength of presence of each other in the home. And we will be able to overcome all the evil that is in the world.

There is so much suffering, so much hatred, so much misery, and we with our prayer, with our sacrifice are beginning at home.

Prayer for a Deceased Person 147

Love begins at home, and it is not how much we do, but how much love we put in the action that we do. It is to God Almighty - how much we do it does not matter, because He is infinite, but how much love we put in that action. How much we do to Him in the person that we are serving.

Some time ago in Calcutta we had great difficulty in getting sugar, and I don't know how the word got around to the children, and a little boy of four years old, Hindu boy, went home and told his parents: I will not eat sugar for three days, I will give my sugar to Mother Teresa for her children. After three days his father and mother brought him to our home. I had never met them before, and this little one could scarcely pronounce my name, but he knew exactly what he had come to do. He knew that he wanted to share his love.

And this is why I have received such a lot of love from you all. From the time that I have come here I have simply been surrounded with love, and with real, real understanding love. It could feel as if everyone in India, everyone in Africa is somebody very special to you. And I felt quite at home I was telling Sister today. I feel in the Convent with the Sisters as if I am in Calcutta with my own Sisters. So completely at home here, right here.

And so here I am talking with you - I want you to find the poor here, right in your own home first. And begin love there. Be that good news to your own people. And find out about your next-door neighbour - do you know who they are? I had the most extraordinary experience with a Hindu family who had eight children.

A gentleman came to our house and said: Mother Teresa, there is a family with eight children, they had not eaten for so long - do something. So I took some rice and I went there immediately. And I saw the children - their eyes shinning with hunger - I don't know if you have ever seen hunger. But I have seen it very often. And she took the rice, she divided the rice, and she went out. When she came back I asked her - where did you go, what did you do? And she gave me a very simple answer: They are hungry also. What struck me most was that she knew - and who are they, a Muslim family - and she knew. I didn't bring more rice that

148 *Mother Teresa*

evening because I wanted them to enjoy the joy of sharing. But there were those children, radiating joy, sharing the joy with their mother because she had the love to give. And you see this is where love begins - at home. And I want you - and I am very grateful for what I have received. It has been a tremendous experience and I go back to India - I will be back by next week, the 15th I hope - and I will be able to bring your love.

And I know well that you have not given from your abundance, but you have given until it has hurt you. Today the little children they have - I was so surprised - there is so much joy for the children that are hungry.

That the children like themselves will need love and care and tenderness, like they get so much from their parents. So let us thank God that we have had this opportunity to come to know each other, and this knowledge of each other has brought us very close.

And we will be able to help not only the children of India and Africa, but will be able to help the children of the whole world, because as you know our Sisters are all over the world. And with this prize that I have received as a prize of peace, I am going to try to make the home for many people that have no home.

Because I believe that love begins at home, and if we can create a home for the poor - I think that more and more love will spread. And we will be able through this understanding love to bring peace, be the good news to the poor. The poor in our own family first, in our country and in the world.

To be able to do this, our Sisters, our lives have to be woven with prayer. They have to be woven with Christ to be able to understand, to be able to share. Because today there is so much suffering - and I feel that the passion of Christ is being relived all over again - are we there to share that passion, to share that suffering of people.

Around the world, not only in the poor countries, but I found the poverty of the West so much more difficult to remove. When I pick up a person from the street, hungry, I give him a plate of rice, a piece of bread, I have satisfied. I have removed that hunger.

Prayer for a Deceased Person 149

But a person that is shut out, that feels unwanted, unloved, terrified, the person that has been thrown out from society - that poverty is so hurtable and so much, and I find that very difficult.

Our Sisters are working amongst that kind of people in the West. So you must pray for us that we may be able to be that good news, but we cannot do that without you, you have to do that here in your country. You must come to know the poor, maybe our people here have material things, everything, but I think that if we all look into our own homes, how difficult we find it sometimes to smile at each, other, and that the smile is the beginning of love.

And so let us always meet each other with a smile, for the smile is the beginning of love, and once we begin to love each other naturally we want to do something.

So you pray for our Sisters and for me and for our Brothers, and for our Co-Workers that are around the world. That we may remain faithful to the gift of God, to love Him and serve Him in the poor together with you.

What we have done we should not have been able to do if you did not share with your prayers, with your gifts, this continual giving. But I don't want you to give me from your abundance, I want that you give me until it hurts.

The other day I received 15 dollars from a man who has been on his back for twenty years, and the only part that he can move is his right hand.

And the only companion that he enjoys is smoking. And he said to me: I do not smoke for one week, and I send you this money. It must have been a terrible sacrifice for him, but see how beautiful, how he shared, and with that money I bought bread and I gave to those who are hungry with a joy on both sides, he was giving and the poor were receiving.

This is something that you and I - it is a gift of God to us to be able to share our love with others. And let it be as it was for Jesus. Let us love one another as he loved us. Let us love Him with undivided love. And the joy of loving Him and each other - let us give now - that Christmas is coming so close. Let us keep that joy of loving Jesus in our hearts. And share that joy with all that

150   *Mother Teresa*

we come in touch with. And that radiating joy is real, for we have no reason not to be happy because we have no Christ with us. Christ in our hearts, Christ in the poor that we meet, Christ in the smile that we give and the smile that we receive. Let us make that one point: That no child will be unwanted, and also that we meet each other always with a smile, especially when it is difficult to smile.

I never forget some time ago about fourteen professors came from the United States from different universities. And they came to Calcutta to our house. Then we were talking about that they had been to the home for the dying. We have a home for the dying in Calcutta, where we have picked up more than 36,000 people only from the streets of Calcutta, and out of that big number more than 18,000 have died a beautiful death.

They have just gone home to God; and they came to our house and we talked of love, of compassion, and then one of them asked me: Say, Mother, please tell us something that we will remember, and I said to them: Smile at each other, make time for each other in your family. Smile at each other. And then another one asked me: Are you married, and I said: Yes, and I find it sometimes very difficult to smile at Jesus because he can be very demanding sometimes.

This is really something true, and there is where love comes - when it is demanding, and yet we can give it to Him with joy. Just as I have said today, I have said that if I don't go to Heaven for anything else I will be going to Heaven for all the publicity because it has purified me and sacrificed me and made me really ready to go to Heaven. I think that this is something, that we must live life beautifully, we have Jesus with us and He loves us. If we could only remember that God loves me, and I have an opportunity to love others as he loves me, not in big things, but in small things with great love, then Norway becomes a nest of love. And how beautiful it will be that from here a centre for peace has been given. That from here the joy of life of the unborn child comes out. If you become a burning light in the world of peace, then really the Nobel Peace Prize is a gift of the Norwegian people. God bless you!.

Prayer for a Deceased Person 151

MOTHER TERESA AND THE INDIANS

But if the Albanians and the Macedonian Slavs are so touched by 'their' Mother Teresa's 'attachment' to them, and therefore entitled to make so much noise about the nun's occasional use of 'my' in reference to Albania and Skopje, then imagine what the Indians could do to 'copyright' her. After all, she spent in India not only a few days, as is the case with Albania, or eighteen years, as in Macedonia's case, but almost seventy successive years.

The long time she spent in India is one of the reasons why Mother Teresa used for her adopted country an endearing diction that she never employed for any other country or people, including 'her' Albanians and Macedonian Slavs. India had fascinated Mother Teresa for some time before she decided to go there as a nun in 1928. She grew even more attached to this vast, fascinating and populous country as soon as she arrived in Calcutta, West Bengal, on 6 January 1929.

From 1948, the year when she left the Loreto order to work in the slums of Calcutta, her identification with India and the Indian people became complete.

In the same eventful year, she replaced the dark habit she had been wearing for twenty years as a European nun, with the white sari of a poor Indian woman.

From 1960, the year she made her first trip outside India, she was always keen to show to the world how much she had absorbed India and Indian culture. The white Catholic nun who always dressed and *namasted* (greeted) her admirers around the world like an Indian, saw herself as a natural international 1 spokeswoman of India and the Indian nation. 'We in India love *our* children,' (emphasis added) she told the national convention of the National Council of Catholic Women in Las Vegas in October 1960.

That Mother Teresa saw herself primarily as an Indian is also obvious from her correspondence with several leaders of India. Her Indianness and devotion to India are seen especially in the letter she sent to the Indian prime minister Morarji Desai and the country's parliamentarians in 1978. In her message, the nun

152 *Mother Teresa*

expresses her concern about 'The Freedom of Religion Bill' proposed in the Indian Parliament. The following are some of the selected excerpts from this long letter. I have italicized the words and phrases that, in my view, reveal her attachment to India and the Indian people:

Dear Mr Desai and Members of *our Parliament,* After much prayer and sacrifices I write to you, asking you to face God in prayer, before you take the step which will destroy the joy and freedom of *our people. Our people,* as you know better than I – are God-fearing people.... I love *my people* very much, more than myself.... *Our people* in Arunachal are so disturbed. All these years *our people* have lived together in peace.... Who are we to prevent *our people* from finding this God who has made them – who loves them – to whom they have to return? You took over your sacred duty in the name of God – acknowledging God's supreme right over *our country* and her people. It was so beautiful. But now I am afraid for you. I am afraid for *our people....* You do not know what abortion has done and is doing to *our people....* Mr Desai and Members of Parliament, in the name of God, do not destroy the Freedom *our country and people* have had, to serve and love God according to their conscience and belief. Do not belittle *our Hindu Religion* saying that *our Hindu poor people* give up their religion for 'a plate of rice'.... I have always made it my rule to co-operate whole-heartedly with the Central and State Governments in all undertakings which are *for the good of our people....* Why are we [Christian missionaries] not with *our poor* in Arunachal?... The Catholics of *our country* have called an All-India day of fasting, prayer and sacri-fice on Friday, 6 April to maintain peace and communal harmony and to ensure that India lives up to its noble tradition of religious freedom. I request you to propose a similar day of intercession for *all communities of our country* – that *we may obtain peace, unity and love;* that *we become one heart,* full of love and so become the sunshine of God's love, the hope of eternal happiness and the burning flame of God's love and compassion, in *our families, our country* and in the world.

(sd.) M. Teresa MC

God bless you.

Prayer for a Deceased Person   **153**

The bill's main target was to restrict the Christian missionaries' activities in India. Mother Teresa was, of course, upset by this, but in her letter she does not speak only on behalf of her religious order, the Christian mission-aries, the Indian Christians or the Christian community in Arunachal Pradesh, which by then had already started suffering the consequences of the Indian government's attempts to keep Christianity in check.

As is obvious from the letter, Mother Teresa's language and tone are not those of an outsider and certainly not of a concerned European tourist, but of a 'native' Indian. The letter is so skilfully peppered with the singular and plural first personal pronouns 'I' and 'we', as well as the possessive adjectives 'my' and 'our', that no politician nor any non-Christian in India would have had any reason to question the author's sincerity or, even worse, accuse her of having a motive other than protecting the civil rights of all Indians, and of praising as well as urging India's politicians to preserve the country's long-standing tradition of religious tolerance.

Mother Teresa's heart-felt plea to prime minister Desai is one of the many passionate letters she addressed to India's leading politicians throughout her long stay in India. Her correspondence with the Indian leaders is yet further proof of her exceptional devotion both to the country and to its people. By the time she wrote the 1978 letter, Mother Teresa was already an important figure in India. A year later, the Nobel Prize added weight to her opinion on an international scale. Even when she became an almost unparalleled media celebrity and the epitome of human compassion, she never ceased considering herself primarily an Indian.

As Anne Sebba rightly notes, although several countries awarded Mother Teresa honorary citizenship, she identified herself most closely with India. Echoing the same sentiment, an Italian nun posted at the Missionaries of Charity home in Skopje, who apparently was baffled by the bickering between the Albanians and the Macedonian Slavs about 'their' Mother Teresa on the eve of the beatification, remarked pointedly that the founder of her religious order felt the strongest affinity with another part of the world entirely. The same nun also declared that Mother Teresa

154   *Mother Teresa*

'felt more Indian than any other citizenship'. Mother Teresa, it appears, was not a very eloquent public speaker but she always knew how to win the hearts and minds of leading politicians and ordinary people in India. The Indians have seen numerous Christian missionaries over the centuries but none like Mother Teresa who declared with pride: 'Ami Bharater Bharat Amar' ('I am Indian and India is mine').

And she obviously meant what she said. After all, she never deserted the Indians in her lifetime and, naturally, chose to be buried in their country.

8 Mother Teresa and Media

People approach Mother Teresa's celebrity status mainly from three different perspectives: subjectivism, structuralism and poststructuralism. The employment of these approaches indicates the complexity of the media icon called Mother Teresa and the 'liquid' nature of the notion of celebrity nowadays. Subjectivists maintain that talent, which eventually leads to fame, is innate and God-given.

In Mother Teresa's case, this attitude is apparent in the numerous books, authorized and unauthorized biographies, pictorial histories, television programmes, films (documentary, feature and animated), plays, novels, poems, paintings, musicals and sculptures that often bear the signature of her friends, colleagues, admirers and supporters all over the world. In the media, this interpretation surfaced when she was first spotted by the Indian Catholic press in Calcutta shortly after she had set up the Missionaries of Charity order in 1950. Referring to this time, the reporter Desmond Doig, an Indian Catholic of Anglo-Irish origin, remarked in 1976 that twenty-seven years earlier he was tipped off by a Catholic functionary and fellow journalist to watch the European nun because 'she's quite extraordinary. She's going to be a saint.'

In the first instance, the myth about Mother Teresa's 'sainted' status was apparently started by Mother Teresa herself, something, which, as will be explained later in this chapter, she came to regret. Mother Teresa always maintained that she received the first call from God to serve the poor some time in 1922 before her twelfth birthday. A quarter of a century later she claimed she was the recipient of another call, which she would refer to as 'the call within a call'. On 10 September 1946, during a train journey she heard God 'calling me. The message was clear. I must leave the convent to help the poor by living among them.' This, Mother

156   *Mother Teresa*

Teresa believed, 'was an order. To fail it would have been to break the faith.'

Even when she became world famous, and was aware that her words were likely to be scrutinized by her friends and foes alike, Mother Teresa would not hesitate to express in public her belief that she was somehow in direct contact with God and the Ancient Fathers of the Church. One of her preferred parables involving herself was the 'encounter' with Saint Peter at heaven's door. Peter had tried to keep her from going in, saying 'I'm sorry. We have no shacks in heaven.' Upset by the doorman saint's 'irreverence', the saint-to-be had responded: 'Very well! I will fill heaven with the people from the slums of the city, and then you will have no other choice than to let me in.'

Mother Teresa accepts that the holy 'encounter' took place when she was delirious and suffering from a very high fever. One does not have to be a psychoanalyst or an atheist to conclude that, like the second call in 1946, her 'audience' with Peter could have been triggered by her poor health and agitated state of mind. Unfortunately, we do not know much about the exact state of Mother Teresa's health when she received the first call. Like most of her first eighteen years in Skopje, even this life-changing incident remains something of a mystery.

What is widely known, though, is that throughout her childhood Mother Teresa was frequently ill and confined to her bed. She suffered from malaria and whooping cough and also had a club foot. Her parents were constantly concerned because of her illnesses, especially her mother who thought 'she would lose her because of her fragile health'. Mother Teresa's health did not get any better in India. She was often sick, especially in 1946. This is what Sister Marie Thérèse recalls about that year: 'We were careful of her. I don't know whether she realized it, but we were.... When it came to the work and the running around, our Superiors took extra care with her.' She was apparently so sick that her friends feared she would be stricken with tuberculosis. As a precaution, she was asked to stay in bed for three hours every afternoon. Seeing no improvement, she was directed to go to the hill station of Darjeeling to recuperate. On the way there the sick and tired

Mother Teresa and Media

Mother Teresa had her second 'encounter' with God. Seen in the context of the Holy Scriptures, Mother Teresa's paranormal experiences are similar to what many prophets, apostles, disciples and saints before her have apparently gone through. Mental anguish and poor health frequently seem to have paved the way to 'revelations'. Jews and Muslims, for instance, maintain that prophets such as Moses and Mohammed suffered from depression when God communicated with them directly.

Different people approach and interpret 'holiness' in different ways. In the case of devout believers, a person's sanctity is measured not so much by their ability to perform miracles as by their absolute faith in the strange ways God works through some chosen individuals. This is one of the key themes in Saint Paul's first letter to the Corinthians:

Now concerning spiritual gifts, brothers and sisters, I do not want you to be uninformed.... Now there are varieties of gifts, but the same Spirit; and there are varieties of services, but the same Lord; and there are varieties of activities, but it is the same God who activates all of them in everyone. To each is given the manifestation of the Spirit for the common good. To one is given through the Spirit the utterance of wisdom, and to another the utterance of knowledge according to the same Spirit, to another faith by the same Spirit, to another gifts of healing by the one Spirit, to another the working of miracles, to another prophecy, to another the discernment of spirits, to another various kinds of tongues, to another the interpretation of tongues.

All these are activated by one and the same Spirit, who allots to each one individually just as the Spirit chooses.... And God has appointed in the church first apostles, second prophets, third teachers; then deeds of power, then gifts of healing, forms of assistance, forms of leadership, 3111 various kinds of tongues. Are all apostles? Are all prophets? Are all teachers? Do all work miracles? Do all possess gifts of healing? Do all speak in tongues? Do all interpret? But strive for the greater gifts. And I will show you a still more excellent way.

Those who are not very religious, on the other hand, are eager to find some more down-to-earth explanations about Mother

158   *Mother Teresa*

Teresa's 'audiences' with God or the Old Fathers of the Church. Failure to provide some rational accounts has shrouded the nun's figure in mysticism and mystery in the eyes of many secular beholders who respect her. While Mother Teresa's religious admirers consider her skill in 'paranormal' commun-4ication as an undeniable proof of her 'divine' nature, others who are not religious and who do not necessarily object to her work and legacy could well perceive it as evidence of mental disturbance.

My intention here is not to approve or disapprove of the opposing interpretations of Mother Teresa's 'paranormal' abilities. Instead, I intend to offer a middle way which will hopefully be useful in approaching her figure and legacy without preconceptions and eventually in helping to clear away the supernatural fog her figure, intentions, work and legacy seem to have been shrouded in for quite some time.

It is my belief that the more details we know about the personal lives of influential people, especially if they are invested with 'supernatural' powers, the easier it will be to answer some of the puzzling questions about them in particular and human nature in general. Considering how much Mother Teresa was immersed in literature (secular and religious) from a young age, her strong ambition to become a writer, and the obvious creative flair she displayed in the poems she wrote in Skopje,and in numerous letters she sent from India to her family and friends in the Balkans from 1929 onwards, it is not difficult to see how the educated, enthusiastic and imaginative young woman, who turned into a devout nun, could have occasionally blurred reality with fantasy, especially when she was suffering from recurring bouts of ill health.

A string of coincidences also seems to have strengthened Mother Teresa's conviction that God intervened to help her in fulfilling her vocation as Jesus's special 'envoy' to alleviate the suffering of the poor. In her speeches, press conferences and books penned by her, or by her admirers on her behalf, she would often mention moments of crisis when things had finally, out of the blue, turned out to be all right. Food, money, clothes and shelter were apparently made available to Mother Teresa and her sisters and

Mother Teresa and Media 159

brothers when most needed and least expected. Mother Teresa never saw such occurrences as mere coincidences. Neither did her supporters and admirers, whose numbers grew as a result of witnessing her 'divine' ability to seek and always secure God's help. As the news about Mother Teresa's extraordinary ability to secure God's intervention for the sake of the poor at the eleventh hour began to spread, she came to be seen as the modern personification of a shamanic figure *par excellence*. Likewise, her determination to *care* for the sick was gradually but steadily perceived and interpreted as a miraculous power to *cure* them. In the Roman Catholic Church, anything belonging to or that has been touched by a saint or a person about to be proclaimed a saint – bones, strands of hair, the remains, vials of blood, burial site, possessions, clothes, books, letters, pictures and statues – is called a 'relic' and is venerated and cherished dearly by their brethren after their death.In Mother Teresa's case, however, her sanctity took root and flourished during her lifetime. Rich and poor, intellectuals and uneducated people, believers and non-believers, Catholics and followers of other faiths who had been in contact with her or had only heard about her were gradu-ally falling under her spell. Mother Teresa's letters and gifts to her admirers were treated by them as 'relics' even while she was alive.

Following her 1968 BBC interview with the journalist Malcolm Muggeridge, the nun's reputation also began to spread across 'secular' and 'rational' Western Europe. Many people who met her in the late 1960s and early 1970s did not know what to make of her. There were some, however, who felt spell-bound in her presence, and their numbers grew throughout the 1980s and 1990s. Stories about Mother Teresa's positive impact on people's lives mushroomed not only among Catholics but also among non-Catholics and the secular-minded. The Mother Teresa 'fan-club', it appears, was and remains a very broad church.

Mother Teresa's opponents, on the other hand, find stories about her 'supernatural' abilities ridiculous and bizarre. They are particularly keen to make fun of the incident involving the controversial BBC journalist Malcolm Muggeridge who in 1969 went to Calcutta to prepare a docu-mentary about Mother Teresa.

160   *Mother Teresa*

Referring to the incident in his 1971 book *Something Beautiful for God: Mother Teresa of Calcutta*, Muggeridge explains that filming inside Nirmal Hriday (Bengali for 'the place of the pure heart'), the Home for the Dying Destitute, which Mother Teresa had founded in Kalighat in 1952, proved problematic because the place was dimly lit. Although he was reluctant, the cameraman Ken Macmillan eventually had a go.

Confident that he would fail to record anything inside the building, Macmillan also took some film outside. But the cameraman had obviously worried in vain. Much to his and Muggeridge's surprise, when the film was processed in London, they noticed that 'the part taken inside was bathed in a particularly beautiful soft light, whereas the part taken outside was rather dim and confused'.Both Muggeridge and Macmillan were delighted with the unexpected result but not for the same reason.

For Macmillan there was no mystery involved. He had taken delivery of some new film made by Kodak shortly before going to Calcutta. This is Macmillan's reaction to the pleasant surprise:

'That's amazing. That's extraordinary.' And I was going to go on to say, you know, three cheers for Kodak. I didn't get a chance to say that though, because Malcolm, sitting in the front row, spun round and said: 'It's divine light! It's Mother Teresa. You'll find that it's divine light, old boy.' And three or four days later I found I was being phoned by journalists from London newspapers who were saying things like: 'We hear you've just come back from India with Malcolm Muggeridge and you were the witness of a miracle.'

Muggeridge did his best to spread the news about the 'miracle'. He was so eager to tell people about his 'divine' experience that it soon turned almost into an obsession. In his own words, '[i]t so delighted me that I fear I talked and wrote about it to the point of tedium, and sometimes of irritation'. But who can blame Muggeridge for getting carried away?

After all, miracles are not daily occurrences, not even for journalists. And since not many people were with him in Calcutta to witness the miraculous event for themselves, Muggeridge naturally saw it as his own sacred duty to describe the paranormal

Mother Teresa and Media 161

encounter as vividly and accurately as possible to humanity at large:

I myself am absolutely convinced that the technically unaccountable light is, in fact, the Kindly Light [Cardinal] Newman refers to in his well-known exquisite hymn.... Mother Teresa's Home for the Dying is overflowing with love, as one senses immediately on entering it. This love is luminous, like the haloes artists have seen and made visible round the heads of the saints. I find it not at all surprising that the luminosity should register on a photographic film. The supernatural is only an infinite projection of the natural, as the furthest horizon is an image of eternity....One thing everyone who has seen the film seems to be agreed about is that the light in the Home for the Dying is quite exceptionally lovely.

This is, from every point of view, highly appropriate. Dying derelicts from the street might normally be supposed to be somewhat repellent, giving off stenches, emitting strange groans. Actually, if the Home for the Dying were piled high with flowers and resounding with musical chants – as it may well have been in its Kali days – it could not be more restful and serene. So, the light conveys perfectly what the place is really like; an outward and visible luminosity mani-festing God's inward and invisible omnipresent love. This is precisely what miracles are for – to reveal the inner reality of God's outward creation. I am personally persuaded that Ken recorded the first authentic photographic miracle.

Muggeridge's interpretation of the 'miracle' and his unashamedly partisan portrayal of Mother Teresa's image and work in his 1969 tele-vision documentary, the 1971 book and numerous interviews undoubtedly heightened his 'celebrity' status. His career as a journalist was also given an unexpected boost. This was hardly surprising. After all, Muggeridge had scooped the 'miracle' story of the twentieth century. It is not very often that a reporter has the chance to offer his contemporaries the oppor-tunity to see with the naked eye what countless generations have hoped for in vain. Not many mortals have been blessed to witness a miracle since Moses split the Red Sea, Jesus walked on

162   *Mother Teresa*

water, and Mohammed ascended to and returned from heaven. Muggeridge must have really felt like the chosen one.

Muggeridge's 'miracle claim' and the noise he made about it caused some embarrassment to the Catholic Church. None the less, the story stuck. Muggeridge the journalist had paved the way for the elevation of Mother Teresa to the position of a 'living saint'. On 29 December 1975, four years after the publication of Muggeridge's saint-making book *Something Beautiful for God*, *Time* magazine accompanied Mother Teresa's portrait on the front cover with the caption 'Messengers of Love and Hope – Living Saints'.

The news about the miracle called Mother Teresa was music to the ears of a largely sceptical, but willing-to-be-deceived, secular Western audi-ence. It is always good to know that we are not a God-forsaken race, that there is still hope for redemption, that we are being looked after by a divine power, that we have the means of finding proof about the exist-ence of our heavenly Father and communicating with him, if not on a one-to-one basis, at least through the mediation of a nun called Mother Teresa.

In 1962 Daniel J. Boorstin remarked:

We need not be theologians to see that we have shifted responsibility for making the world interesting from God to the newspaperman. We used to believe there were only so many 'events' in the world. If there were not many intriguing or startling occurrences, it was no fault of the reporter. He could not be expected to report what did not exist.In a way, the newspaperman has been reporting 'what did not exist' since the dawn of the modern press. Reporting the real and the unreal, or what Boorstin calls 'pseudo-events', was a seminal feature of the news industry from the start. Boorstin rightly laments that 'pseudo-events' seem to have taken over, but he apparently did not foresee the extraordinary length some journalists would go to and the sources and the means they would employ to 'invent' them.

In the case of the 'divine light' recorded in the Home for the Dying, we apparently discovered yet another potential of the media: the ability to produce miraculous pseudo-events. If God was indeed dead, thanks to modern technologies we could reincarnate him, and if he never existed in the first place, we can

Mother Teresa and Media 163

literally invent him. Apparently, we have not only the mental gift to imagine miracles but also the means to materialize them. Technology obviously does not necessarily make myths distant and irrelevant. On the contrary, it manufactures them as commodities that are increasingly in demand.

As Christopher Hitchens puts it, 'modern technology and communications have ensured... that rumour and myth can be transmitted with ever greater speed and efficiency to the eyes and ears of the credulous'.

The fact that Mother Teresa herself was instrumental in creating the myth about her 'paranormal' abilities does not necessarily belittle the significance of her work in Calcutta. Nor does the endorsement of her saint-like status by devout Catholics and a 'sensationalist' journalist like Muggeridge make her lifetime devotion to Jesus and to the poor less appealing to millions of people who do not necessarily believe in miracles allegedly recorded by Kodak. If Mother Teresa's saintly nature is a matter for debate, her commitment to her vocation and to the poor was exemplary.

This is one of the reasons why the Indian media, both Catholic and non-Catholic, were keen to support and advertise her work from the start. And not only the Indian media. From the 1950s onwards, many leaders in West Bengal and India were willing and eager to fully endorse and sponsor Mother Teresa's brand of charity work. Politicians such as the Chief Minister of West Bengal Dr Bidhan Chandra Roy and Indian prime ministers like Jawaharlal Nehru and his daughter Indira Gandhi would often employ the Bengali and Indian press to put and keep Mother Teresa constantly in the spotlight.

Thanks to numerous Indian leaders' direct interest in her, the Indian political establishment and the Indian media acknowledged Mother Teresa as a 'living saint' before she caught the lenses of the European and American media, even before the miraclespotter Muggeridge.

In July 1961 Mother Teresa made headlines in the Indian press thanks to her good friend Dr Roy. Interviewed on his eightieth birthday, the senior and much respected politician surprised his

164 *Mother Teresa*

fellow countrymen by the unexpected tribute he paid to the Catholic nun. 'As I climbed the steps of the Writers' Buildings leading to my office,' he told a *Calcutta Statesman* reporter, 'I was thinking of Mother Teresa who devotes her life to the service of the poor.'

The same paper commented that 'Dr Roy felt that Mother Teresa was doing magnificent work. She served those who were most miserable and found no place in hospitals, and among them were lepers and cholera patients.' Asked by a Christian audience in the late 1960s what he thought of Mother Teresa, Dr Zakir Hussain, the Muslim president of India, replied: 'In your lexicon I believe this woman is a saint.'

Mother Teresa's 'saintly' nature was also apparently acknowledged by less distinguished Indians. One of the parables most frequently mentioned by Mother Teresa's admirers regarding the difficulties she encountered in her work at the beginning of her religious order is about an incident which occurred at the Homef ort heD yings hortlyaf teri tw aso pened.H avingr eceived complaints from fanatic Hindus that the patients who died in the home, which was set up in the two halls adjoining Calcutta's famous temple in Kalighat, were baptized by Mother Teresa's sisters in their final moments and then buried as Christians, the city's Chief Medical Officer and a senior police officer went there to investigate the issue for themselves.

The story goes that the officers found Mother Teresa so engrossed in her work that it took her some time to notice them. When she eventually became aware of their presence, she offered to show them her work, an offer which the Indian officials politely declined. Turning to the crowd of Hindu believers who were waiting in anticipation outside, the police officer is reported to have said: 'Yes, I will send this woman away, but only after you have persuaded your mothers and sisters to come here to do the work that she is doing. This woman is a saint.'

The Indians have a long-established veneration for holiness. They hold in especially high esteem those who devote themselves to others. This explains to some extent why those Indians who came to know Mother Teresa in person, were familiar with her work and helped her in any way they could, had no hesitation in

Mother Teresa and Media 165

taking to their hearts a white woman and a Catholic missionary. They acknowledged and appreciated from the first her selflessness and devotion to the poor, the orphans, the old and the infirm, who had been abandoned by their families and ignored by neighbours. The local Indians did not need the intervention of politicians or the intrusion of the media to be convinced that Mother Teresa was 'one of them'. In his 2005 collection *The Argumentative Indian: Writings on Indian History, Culture and Identity*, Bengali-born Nobel Prize-winning econ-omist Amartya Sen attributes India's ability to accommodate different faiths, cultures, traditions and customs mainly to his country's rich argu-mentative tradition.

This could well be the case but, like every other civilization past and present, India and Hinduism also have a long tradi-tion of intolerance both towards the 'native other' and towards foreigners. Hindus, like Ancient Greeks, have traditionally looked down upon aliens. In the words of the renowned Indian diplomat, writer and columnist Pavan K. Varma:

The violence and bigotry traditionally inflicted by high-caste Hindus on members of their own faith, the low-caste Shudras, has no parallel in any other religion. Nor is Hinduism particularly welcoming to outside influences. We need only recall that until recently Hindus considered all foreigners to be *mleccha*, inherently unclean, and regarded those who ventured to foreign lands – as Mahatma Gandhi famously did when he left for England to study law in 1888 – as having polluted themselves.For a foreigner like Mother Teresa to have made friends among Indians of all faiths, especially Hindus, from the start of her lonely venture into the slums of Calcutta is proof of her humility and ability to convince her Indian acquaintances and friends that, although a stranger, she had their best interests at heart.

The nun's success also proves the Indians' gratitude to outsiders like her who are always sensitive to local culture and tradition. Mother Teresa may not have been as well-known and admired across all sections of Indian society as her staunch supporters often maintain in their writings, but those who knew and backed her certainly respected her as one of their own. More importantly, such helpful people did not expect any public recognition for their

166   *Mother Teresa*

support. Their cooperation with Mother Teresa was unconditional. Some of India's political and civic leaders also showed a keen interest in Mother Teresa from the start of her religious congregation in 1950. Indian politicians at local and national level were interested in ensuring that the 'saintly' Mother Teresa was known by as many people as possible in Calcutta and throughout India. It was equally important that the news about her was spread around the world. The leaders of India could see the value of presenting the nun as a foreign 'saint' among the 'welcoming' and 'open-minded' Indians and they used the media very effectively to achieve their aims.

Their efforts were soon to produce dividends. The Catholic nun proved very helpful to the political establishment in India in the wake of independence from Britain and separation from Pakistan in 1947, and the civil war that led to the creation of Bangladesh in 1971. Through Mother Teresa, Indian politicians aimed at highlighting the new India's 'secularism' and promoting the Indians as a tolerant and welcoming nation. Likewise, successive Indian governments backed by the Indian media used Mother Teresa to push forward with their progressive reforms at home to better the lives of millions of citizens traditionally abandoned and shunned by the class-conscious and caste-ridden Indian society.

Them essageo ft heI ndianp oliticiansw hos upportedM other Teresa to their conservative countrymen could not have been any clearer: if a white Western woman, a Roman Catholic nun, could show so much love and affection for India's abandoned children, lepers, untouchables and the dying old, Indians too were surely capable of finding enough love, compas-sion and tolerance in their hearts to show the same noble sentiments. After all, Mother Teresa was hardly saying or doing something the Indians themselves had not heard or done before.

With her charity work, she was rendering her contribution, small as it was, towards keeping alive a not-much-publicized Calcuttan and Indian tradition furthered by 'home-grown' humanists like the 1913 Nobel Prize laureate for literature Rabindranath Tagore, Mahatma Gandhi (another great twentieth century media icon), and several of her contemporaries such as

Mother Teresa and Media 167

Pandurang Shashtri Athavale and Acharya Shri Chandananji. In the words of an Indian journalist in the late 1970s, Mother Teresa and her Sisters:

with their serene ways, their saris, their knowledge of local languages... have come to symbolise not only the best in Christian charity, but also the best in Indian culture and civilisation, from Buddha to Gandhi, the greatest saints, the seers, the great lovers of humanity with boundless compassion and consideration for the underprivileged: what Shakespeare called the 'quality of mercy'.

The founding fathers of modern India aimed at building what Jawaharlal Nehru, the country's first prime minister, called in his 'tryst with destiny' speech to the Constituent Assembly in New Delhi on 14 August 1947, 'the noble mansion of free India where all her children may dwell'. This, Nehru believed, could be achieved by taking and fulfilling the pledge that '[t]he service of India means the service of the millions who suffer. It means the ending of poverty and ignorance and disease and inequality of opportunity'. This was a noble sentiment and a praiseworthy ambition but also a rather tall order in a country where poverty has traditionally been seen as a deserved punishment for a sinful existence in a previous life and as an opportunity for the rich to gain points through almsgiving. Dealing with and eroding the entrenched Indian caste system was a chal-lenge the new leaders of India had to tackle very carefully because they did not want, nor could they afford, to alienate powerful sections of Indian society.

In India, however, the 'segregation' and 'discrimination' of human beings are not allegedly endorsed only by Hinduism. Like the Hindus, a large number of followers of Christianity and Islam across India have traditionally been in favour of the caste system. India will become a 'noble mansion' for all its citizens when the caste system that treats at least one third of the country's population as less than human comes to an end.

The negative impact of the caste system was obvious to the leaders of new India in the second half of the twentieth century. Getting rid of the caste system was undoubtedly a mammoth task, which Nehru and other politicians of his generation, including the

168   *Mother Teresa*

Bengali Communists who reigned in Calcutta for most of the last quarter of the twentieth century and who are still in power, were aware that they could not accomplish. They were also adamant that they would not be able to tackle this issue on their own. This is the reason why they were eager from the first to use whatever help they could get, even from abroad, and from anyone who was sensible enough to tread carefully in the new, complicated political-nationalistic-religious reality of India.

This is where Mother Teresa proved very useful to the emerging post-independence Indian political establishment, and where she excelled from the first. The tact with which she dealt with sensitive issues relating to Indian politics, religions, customs and tradition won her the increasing backing of several Indian leaders and of those sections of the Indian media that were open minded and courageous enough to promote and offer support publicly to a white woman and a Roman Catholic nun at a time when any foreigner or foreign influence was frowned upon. It was mainly thanks to this home support from rank and file Indians, as well as friends in high places, that Mother Teresa came to be seen throughout India as the embodiment of 'love', which St Paul defines in his first letter to the Corinthians as the 'still more excellent way'. In the late 1960s and throughout the 1970s Mother Teresa became the personification of human compassion not only in India but also throughout the world.

Millions of people, irrespective of their colour, creed, nationality, social status, political beliefs and financial position, apparently saw in her work the answer to some of their problems. The nun, it appears, came to be regarded as a modern sage who had found a purpose in life which had nothing to do with materialistic values. Through her much publicized simple life, her strong faith in God, her belief in the goodness of human nature, her humanitarian work and her veneration for life, many people in India and especially in the West seemed to have discovered for themselves a new purpose in life.

In a materialistic world, many apparently believed they had to be grateful to Mother Teresa for showing them a different and equally satisfying way of living. Western individualism and

Mother Teresa and Media   169

materialism were single-handedly challenged by a tiny and unpretentious nun who became an idol for the poor as well as for the rich, for believers as well as non-believers. That such a 'saint' could flourish in India was an excellent advertisement for the new India and her new leaders whose pride in their country did not turn them into blinkered nationalists eager to shun any good foreign influence that could help them in their efforts to set the country on the course of economic and social progress and emancipation.

To Mother Teresa's good fortune, chief minister Roy and prime minister Nehru did not seek to hide their country's problems; nor did they see poverty as an Indian stigma that had to be kept away from the eyes of the world, especially of the colonial West. Mother Teresa was lucky to start her charity work and religious order at a time when West Bengal and India were governed by open-minded leaders who were great Indian patriots with an internationalist vision. It was no coincidence that in his famous 1947 speech Nehru spoke of taking 'the pledge of dedication to India and her people and to the still larger cause of humanity'. If a Western 'saint' could facilitate their work at home as well as improve the image of India abroad, then so be it. This explains, to some extent, why a foreign Christian became a celebrity in India and why she enjoyed such unprece-dentedly high levels of support for so long.

If Mother Teresa was a natural pragmatist, her influential Indian backers obviously never lagged far behind her. In this give-and-take silent pact the 'saint' and the Indian 'saint-makers' from the fields of politics, media, religion and business were all winners. For everyone concerned this seemed like a perfect match. Like any match, however, it did not have the blessing of everyone.

Bibliography

Allegri, Renzo: *Conversations with Mother Teresa: A Personal Portrait of the Saint.* 2011.

Alpion, Gezmin: *Mother Teresa: Saint or Celebrity?.* Routledge Press, 2007.

Chawla, Navin: *Mother Teresa.* Rockport, Mass: Element Books, 1996.

Clucas, Joan: *Mother Teresa.* New York: Chelsea House, 1988.

Graff, Clucas, Joan: *Mother Teresa.* New York. Chelsea House Publications, 1988.

Langford, Joseph: *Mother Teresa's Secret Fire: The Encounter That Changed Her Life, and How It Can Transform Your Own.* Our Sunday Visitor Publishing. 2008.

Le Joly, Edward: *Mother Teresa of Calcutta.* San Francisco: Harper & Row, 1983.

Meg Greene: *Mother Teresa: A Biography,* Greenwood Press, 2004.

Sebba, Anne: *Mother Teresa: Beyond the Image.* New York. Doubleday, 1997.

Spink, Kathryn: *Mother Teresa: A Complete Authorized Biography.* New York. HarperCollins, 1997.

Williams, Paul: *Mother Teresa.* Indianapolis. Alpha Books, 2002.

Index

A
Achievements, 28, 55.

B
Baptisms, 23, 62.
Beatification, 6, 10, 11, 30, 31, 70, 71, 100, 153.

C
Catholic Church, 1, 21, 33, 62, 72, 77, 91, 95, 139, 141, 159, 162.
Charitable Activities, 39, 43, 64.
Commemorations, 33, 67.

D
Deceased Person, 135.
Donations, 4, 20, 21, 26, 39, 59, 65.

F
Foundation, 12, 58, 99.

G
Government, 22, 27, 34, 39, 43, 53, 55, 60, 62, 78, 79, 80, 90, 106, 120, 122, 123, 129, 130, 132.

I
International Charity, 5, 40.

J
Jesus, 5, 13, 14, 16, 26, 28, 29, 46, 47, 48, 49, 50, 51, 54, 88, 100, 101, 103, 104, 106, 132, 133, 134, 135, 136, 137, 138, 139, 140, 141, 142, 143, 146, 149, 150, 161, 163.

M
Media, 26, 27, 61, 63, 66, 69, 71, 72, 77, 105, 110, 111, 112, 113, 114, 117, 131, 137, 153, 155, 162, 163, 165, 166, 168, 169.
Medical Care, 15, 27, 64, 65, 66.
Memorial Museum, 89.
Miracle, 1, 23, 30, 31, 160, 161, 162.
Missionaries of Charity, 1, 3, 4, 5, 6, 13, 18, 19, 20, 21, 22, 27, 30, 33, 40, 41, 43, 44, 45, 46, 47, 53, 54, 58, 59, 60, 65, 66, 67, 68, 74, 78, 93, 94, 95, 96, 97, 98, 99, 100, 101, 103, 104, 106, 107, 108, 111, 138, 147, 148, 149, 151, 164, 168.
Motivation, 64.
Musical Tribute, 90.

172

Mother Teresa

O
Organizations, 64.

P
Policy, 116, 119, 121, 122, 123, 126, 127, 128.
Popular Culture, 33.
Prayers, 11, 48, 49, 109, 132, 149.

Q
Questionable Relationships, 63.

R
Racism, 65, 128.

Religious Calling, 36, 37.
Religious Life, 2, 38, 49, 59, 81, 99, 107, 132, 136.

S
Saint Teresa, 101.
Spiritual Life, 28.
Supreme Court, 131.

V
Violence, 2, 131, 138, 165.

W
Witness, 7, 8, 9, 101, 105, 106, 131, 139, 141, 160, 161.
Woman Deceased, 49.

❑❑❑

CPSIA information can be obtained
at www.ICGtesting.com
Printed in the USA
FSOW02n1147150116
15840FS